CARRIER
TO
Classroom

CHARLES W. BALDWIN

ISBN:978-1-4834-7111-2 (sc)
ISBN: 978-1-4834-7113-6 (hc)
ISBN: 978-1-4834-7112-9 (e)

Library of Congress Control Number: 2017909321

Lulu Publishing Services rev. date: 6/30/2017

FOREWORD

I have known many strong, high energy leaders over my 34 years in the Navy and nearly 20 in industry, but Chuck Baldwin is unique. His combination of strong character, high energy, confidence, vision, loyalty and sheer enthusiasm combined with his jaunty and always upbeat personality are seldom encountered in senior enlisted leaders (or in flag officers, for that matter). I have followed his work closely over the decades since I first met him. I watched with admiration as he set a new high standard for *the* most challenging senior enlisted leadership job in the Navy, that of Command Master Chief on a nuclear aircraft carrier. During that tour, he earned the respect of the entire crew and wardroom with his strong leadership, deep command loyalty, creative energy, and wise counsel. I was surprised and disappointed when he chose to retire after that adventure. I didn't want to lose him as an active duty shipmate but I learned pretty quickly that there were even more challenging and important jobs in store for him.

Within a year after his leaving the Navy, I visited him at his first teaching job and spoke to his cadets and observed that as a Naval Science instructor he had found his niche for the next phase of life, molding the lives of young cadets in high school Naval Junior Reserve Officer Programs (NJROTC).

Later, when we were hiking the trails of Shenandoah National Park together, our discussions revealed that he was not fully satisfied as an instructor but longed to accomplish more and bigger things. He told me then that he was planning to "build my own high school" that would set new standards in every area of secondary education as well as recruiting and preparing young men and women for success in military service. I marveled at his outsized dreams, but I had my doubts; I had never known anyone who "built their own high school."

So, imagine my surprise and delight when only a few years later I visited Delaware Military Academy (DMA) and walked the halls of the first buildings with him and his staff of hand-picked teachers and hundreds of uniformed cadets. I listened to Chuck describe the school's achievements and praise his teachers and students. As he detailed his vision with near manic enthusiasm, I no longer doubted anything he planned or imagined. And it's a good thing I didn't, because under his leadership as Commandant (principal) the campus grew, academic and athletic programs were added, expanded and improved at record rates, and DMA cadets set new standards in every area of secondary education.

After a decade, when DMA's campus was complete and a half dozen classes had graduated, Chuck chose to retire. He had much to be proud of. His cadets were high school graduates equipped to succeed in life. They had gone to college, trade school or entered the workforce with confidence. Some went on to the Naval Academy, West Point, the Air Force Academy and college ROTC programs, or they were well along in enlisted career tracks or a myriad of civilian trades. Most important, they were good citizens, responsible and patriotic.

Not surprisingly, Chuck found retirement unsatisfying and completely lacking in the challenges he thrived on. He had more big dreams; dreams of expanding the Junior ROTC program further and helping underprivileged youngsters escape their environment and become high achieving citizens.

In *Carrier to Classroom*, Chuck's experience and wisdom is communicated in pithy, hard-hitting style. Mixing sea stories and proverbs of his own making, he effectively communicates an intimate understanding of the myriad challenges of teaching youngsters, communicating with parents and leading staff. Knowledge and understanding gained over his years on the deck plates of Navy ships and in the high school environment is translated into wise counsel.

His advice is not complicated. It is neither conventional nor radical. Rather, it is thoughtful and minimalist, and it's based on success that is backed by hard data. In dealing with students, he stresses the importance of discipline, but also commends forgiveness instead of punishment and thoughtful situational discretion versus lock-step adherence to fixed guidelines. I read something in the news almost every week that indicates this kind of common sense discretion is entirely missing in many of today's public schools.

My only disappointment in this book is that it is not longer. It is certain that he has much more worth sharing, so let's hope this is remedied by a second book. In the meantime, I am satisfied that *Carrier to Classroom* will soon be found in the hands of educators across this country, benefiting teachers, administrators, parents and students.

Carrier to Classroom is directed at those leaving military service; it is intended to inspire them to take their values, energy and experience into the classroom, but It is my fervent hope that it also finds its way into the hands of governors, lawmakers at every level, school boards and superintendents and parents. There is a desperate need for the lessons of the Delaware Military Academy to be learned and put into place across our nation. After more than 20 years of high achievement in Delaware secondary education, it is past time for his vision to spread nationwide and contribute to a renaissance in secondary education.

The overt message in this book is an appeal to the military veteran to join Chuck in the battle, but there is also an equally clear message to all involved in education or concerned about our youth. And that message is "we can and must do better."

Master Chief Petty Officer of the Navy, Ret., John Hagan

Charles Baldwin is one of the most accomplished leaders in our lifetime. Serving the country as a Navy Command Master Chief, he earned the respect of men and women with whom he worked as well as that of the American people whom he served.

As an education leader, Chuck has been a visionary, inspiring educators to support all students in their journey to become informed and productive citizens. His lifelong commitment to service has been exemplary and his passion for excellence has positively impacted the lives of thousands of youth, their parents and families.

As a colleague and friend, Chuck has enriched my professional as well as my personal life and our work together in the education arena has been some of the most productive and fun times of my career.

Robert J. Andrzejewski, Ed.D.
Teacher and retired Superintendent of Schools, Red Clay Consolidated and Christina School Districts, Delaware

Chuck (aka Charles, Master Chief, Carlo, Commandant, and Mr. Baldwin) is one of those rare individuals who truly brightens the world around them. His life is a testament to and shining example of how one person can meaningfully and positively change the lives of so many others. With careers in the military, education, private enterprise, and government, Chuck has continually demonstrated his exceptional ability to motivate and inspire people while also instilling discipline, structure, and purpose. Members of the military, educators, school administrators, and business leaders would do themselves a great service by reading his book. It's written in a tone that isn't heavy, nor is it boring. Like interacting with Chuck in person, you come away feeling inspired about life and your potential while also having some clear action items and plans to carry out.

My own story with Chuck starts way back in the summer of 1994. I was at high school pre-season soccer practice before the school year began. I saw this guy in a crisp white military uniform (which I later learned is "summer whites") covered with a chest full of ribbons walk out onto the field to speak with the coach. A moment later I heard, "Tommy, come over here," from the coach. As I irritatedly walked over and shook out my glorious shoulder-length hair, my first words to Chuck were "yeah, man, what do you want?" in a nasty and "over it" tone that only a teenager could muster. Thus began my tutelage. My high school was going to start an NJROTC unit that coming school year, and they had to build out the organizational structure of the students in the battalion. Through luck and hard work, though not intended towards this goal, I had hit the life lottery and was selected to be the Battalion Commander, where I would receive daily instruction and mentoring from Master Chief Chuck Baldwin (and would have to cut off that hair).

After high school, I attended Purdue University (Go Boilermakers!) on a Navy ROTC scholarship with the recommendation from Chuck. Now, I won't say that I exhibited amazing human and leadership behaviors at all (or even most) times during undergrad, but I continued to receive mentoring and guidance from Chuck as I refined my thoughts, perspectives, and philosophies on leadership and management. At all times, Chuck was a positive spirit continually giving me nudges in the right direction when I needed them. In May 2000, as I received my commission as a U.S. Naval Officer, Chuck traveled to Indiana and was my "first salute," which is a time-honored tradition and an honor for me personally.

Over the next five years I embarked on a fantastic active duty journey. This is where all of Chuck's mentorship over the years really started to pay dividends and where the stakes were real. Junior military officers are immediately thrown in the deep end of the pool. They find themselves in charge of people who have greater technical knowledge, more professional experience, and are often older. That can be a disaster if not approached correctly. Chuck's advice and lessons helped me walk the fine line of humility, asking for help (both functionally and in learning how to lead) from my senior enlisted team members while also making it clear that the buck stopped with me. As the years went by and I found myself in tough leadership situations or career decision points, I always went to Chuck for advice. And I always came away feeling uplifted and with either a plan or the beginnings of one.

That chapter closed, and I've since gone on to earn an MBA and a career in the corporate world. The lessons and mentoring from Chuck continue, though now often over a cold beverage—unless we're at Everest base camp, in which case maybe it's a hot lemon tea.

Here's the scoop as I've experienced and learned: It doesn't matter whether you're an E4, E9, O1, or O7, the leadership lessons you learn and apply in the military apply everywhere. The world is full of people looking for others to lead, to provide discipline, structure, a clear vision, and a higher purpose. That is universal.

Our world's education systems are in dire need of teachers and administrators who possess those skills and that passion. My wife, my mother, and all three of my sisters teach or have taught at all levels of education from primary through secondary to higher education. I listen to them and their friends talk about how one of the most difficult things to do right now, and the area where many teachers are lacking, is classroom management and discipline. Military experience most certainly translates and can help in this area.

I'm super excited that Chuck wrote this book. Whether it's

military members transitioning into the classrooms or teachers gaining some tools and a different perspective on leading and managing students, I look forward to seeing the many fruits this book and its lessons will bear for kids around the world.

Thank you, Chuck, for sticking with me, helping to shape me into a better human being, and for ensuring that I picked the service with the most lenient hair-length regulations. The next drink is on me.

Former Student
Tom Hutchison, LCDR USNR IRR, Adventurer, Engineer, Corporate Leader, and former student

> *I love schools, public traditional, public charter, private, parochial, and even home schools. Any person dedicated to educating young people is my hero. Whatever I have to share that may be of use to my colleagues I give freely, along with my respect and admiration.*
>
> *--- Charles Baldwin*

INTRODUCTION

In June of 1968 I marched smartly across the stage and received my high school diploma, with not a clue as to what was next. I had had enough of school and never considered college. It was a coin toss as to whether I would work in one of the local factories or enter military service. Although Vietnam was raging, it seemed preferable to 40 years of schlepping water heaters and silos for AO Smith Harvestore. My father was stuck in such a rut and wanted much more for his little guy.

Having served in the Navy before WWII and in the Merchant Marines during the war, he developed a love for shipboard life. Dad's sea stories were fantastic. Navy it was! I reported to our local recruiter and was off to basic training at Great Lakes, Illinois.

In school I was an extremely good follower and a fair number 2 guy, but never the leader. My skill at plausible deniability was acquired at a very young age. Just spelling leadership was a challenge, let alone understanding all it entailed. The 25-year journey I was about to set sail on would build me into an exceptional leader and prepare me for an even more enjoyable career in education. Learning to communicate with young people, leading by example, moral courage, doing the right thing, and accepting responsibility were everyday events, and I quickly understood the value of honing those skills. Most important, the Navy core values of Honor, Courage, and

Commitment became a lifestyle that gave me the opportunity to enjoy success in my professional and personal life.

My story is one of transferring this hands-on leadership training provided by the U.S. Navy into the public-charter school system. I believe all military personnel at the completion of their service have in them the foundation to enter studies leading to a successful career in education. Classroom management, discipline, budgets, political environment—all things related to the school system are in their tool box. The only exception is certification of their expertise and education in a chosen field of study.

This is not to say only teachers with military experience are the best qualified, but they do indeed have advantages as they develop professionally.

I will also present to you a case for adapting new learning styles, specifically Project Based Learning (PBL) and where and how to participate in successful funding opportunities to support PBL and minor capital projects. Money always seems to be an issue and I have uncovered the jewel of the crowdfunding organizations, USEED—seeding your own project by creating a new level of philanthropy.

Education, in my mind, is the most rewarding and exciting vocation. I, who had enough of education after high school, have now devoted the last 25 years to our public school system. Unfortunately, I had to step aside as a principal several years ago due to an ailment and step into a more behind-the-scenes role as an advisor. I tell you, it was, and is, the absolute worst feeling. I miss the interaction with the students and faculty and working in an environment where "aha moments" are the order of the day.

With that preamble, I sincerely hope you enjoy and perhaps learn something from my journey.

CONTENTS

The military teaches respect and leadership, and those skills are essential in education. But many principals and teachers without military background never learned these lessons. Therefore, military leaders are needed in our schools.

Good leadership is being visible so subordinates can share their concerns with you. But many poor leaders isolate themselves. Therefore, make yourself visible and get to know your students.

Strong, positive school culture is the most important factor for success, and principals and teachers are the most important determinants of their school's culture. But most schools invest little or nothing in leadership development among staff. Therefore, all principals and teachers should receive leadership training.

The answer to every one of the world's problems is education, and the business community is a huge beneficiary of successful education. But funding is always short and business and education operate in silos. Therefore, tell your story to and attract money from the private sector.

Discipline is important for students to have self-respect and respect for others. But students are adolescents and there will be conflict. Therefore, provide leadership, counsel, and treat your students with respect.

You should get to know your students and befriend them. But you will be advised not to befriend them. Therefore, engage with your students in an appropriate manner.

Moral courage and authority are important to you as a responsible faculty member. But in public schools you may have responsibility without authority. Therefore, school boards should support the faculty with authority and responsibility.

Students need to learn to integrate disciplines and become problem solvers. But school systems are resistant to change. Therefore, for impact, implement innovative and 21st century curricula that present students with real life problem-solving experiences.

Parent and business community engagement is enriching to the student experience. But most schools fail to make it easy or inviting for them to participate. Therefore, you should make it easy and inviting for parents and business to collaborate with students.

JROTC is an exciting adventure for both instructors and cadets. But off-campus experiences that take advantage of military bases and resources are expensive. Therefore, you must be creative and engage the community, the military, and veterans organizations to assist with training opportunities.

Success may be achieved in small steps. But most people lack a mindset on how to take the small steps. Therefore, be a risk taker, develop a strategic plan, then tackle your dreams.

It is necessary to have the tools and innovative challenges for students. But resources are scarce. Therefore, connect with your community to find real world problems for students to solve and request their assistance in obtaining material support.

Students want to learn and be successful and need structure and role models. But many school personnel lack experience in constructive discipline. Therefore, veterans are desperately needed to provide leadership, structure and friendship to navigate students toward positive outcomes.

Enthusiasm for helping others and appreciation for intrinsic rewards can offset the sometimes cumbersome bureaucracy.

Several letters from students, parents and fellow educators like those you can look forward to receiving when you make the decision to enter the world of education.

CHAPTER 1

· · · · · · · · · ● · · · · · · · · · · ·

Welcome Aboard Ship/School

Deckplate Leadership is the art of hands-on direction by caring for and respecting your people, leading by example, demonstrating moral courage by doing what is right, not what is popular, and, most important, by being seen and being approachable.

Charles Baldwin

I reported to Great Lakes Naval Training Center on October 10, 1968, and the adventure in the Navy and introduction to leadership began immediately.

After several weeks of sitting back and observing, and of course being screamed at, I noticed that recruits who worked hard and volunteered for duties were being promoted and afforded benefits that seemed to make their lives somewhat easier. Of course, in '68 the most critical and enjoyable of these benefits was additional smoke breaks (imagine that in 2017). So, I became one of the go-to people.

Now, many former service members will advise you to never volunteer for any duty. In fact, they believe NAVY is an acronym for Never Again Volunteer Yourself. **Deckplate Leadership lesson (DPL) number 1: Always accept challenging situations and be known as the one who gets the job done**.

After adopting this attitude, I actually began to enjoy my training experience. And then came week 5, and an encounter with leadership lesson number 2 in regard to following orders.

Week 5 is known as "Service Week"; it requires all members of your recruit company to work at various locations around the base—Drill Hall, Administration, Gymnasium, and the dreaded Mess Hall. Naturally, I drew the Mess Hall. It was dreaded due to the hours, which began at 0330 (3:30 a.m.) and ended at 1930 (7:30 p.m.).

There were 12 serving lines and we fed more than 10,000 recruits at each meal. Identified as a hard worker and one who could be relied upon, I was assigned as line captain on one of the serving lines—my first leadership position. There were eight recruits assigned to a line and my responsibility was to ensure the line was fully stocked, to oversee serving, to authorize breaks, and make sure the dining area was cleaned after each meal. I took my responsibilities seriously and rapidly gained favor with the stew burners (Navy cooks).

One morning at breakfast I had to go through the hardest leadership lesson ever. At each meal the head cook, known in the Navy as the Jack O' the Dust, would inspect, set serving spoons at each station, and identify the appropriate ration. On this particular morning, he placed a very small ladle for the pancake syrup. After he had gone we began to serve and there were numerous complaints as to the dribble of syrup we were providing. I looked at the ladle and, believing the head cook had made an error, I replaced the ladle with one much larger, thus unknowingly changing the ration without authorization. The complaining stopped, but we were going through quite a bit of syrup, requiring me to send runners every few minutes to restock. The Jack O' the Dust came to my line and demanded to know why we were using so much syrup. I really didn't have a good answer.

Then he saw the ladle. "Who authorized this size ladle?" he shouted. I stepped up and said I thought he had made an error with the original size and replaced it myself. He grabbed me by the ear and pulled me into his office.

Once inside he broke out a large regulation manual (the larger the scarier) and had me read a passage indicating unauthorized changing of the ration was a court martial offense. Then he had me stand at attention in front of his desk and called for a Marine guard. Back in the day the Marines were in charge of the Navy brig (jail). Brigs were known for harsh discipline and a tour in the brig usually spelled the end of a Navy career. The Marine looked me square in the eye and said he would return after the evening meal to take me to the brig and deal with my insubordination. Shaken, I reported back to my line to continue my duties.

Great, five weeks into the Navy and I managed to really screw up. No traveling around the world for me, just the lock-up. All day long I worried and as the time arrived for me to report to the office, I had a terrible feeling in the pit of my stomach.

When I arrived at his office at 1900, the Jack O' Dust had me stand at attention and asked if I had thought about what I had done. I had indeed. He informed me of **DPL number 2: It is okay to question an order, but proper procedure is to report your concern to your superiors before taking action.** If I had done that, and a mistake had been made, it could have been corrected without draining Vermont of maple syrup.

Then a Marine—a sergeant—came in, and I was sure my Navy adventure was about to come to an end. He asked me to face the bulkhead (wall) and stand at attention. He wondered aloud if I had given thought to my actions, and I indicated in the affirmative. He then kicked me in the behind and I jumped about two feet. Once I landed he told me to get out of his sight, think about my actions, return to my barracks and never report to him again. I assured him there was no problem there and I was gone in a flash.

I certainly do not condone any physical violence, but I must admit it was one of the best kicks in the butt I've ever received. To this day, I eat pancakes and waffles dry.

The next major event in my leadership evolution occurred 18 months after basic training, in the Republic of Vietnam. Prior to my reporting to Vietnam, the Navy had assigned me to Port Hueneme, California, for two weeks of five-ton truck driving school followed by one week of SERE (Survival, Evasion, Resistance, Escape) training.

After arriving in Saigon, I reported to the Annapolis Hotel Barracks downtown to await my final destination. After several days, I was assigned to Naval Support Activity Detachment Cat Lo, located some 60 miles southeast of Saigon, near the city of Vung Tau, on the South China Sea. Since I was in a war zone, my assignment could have been much worse. We were a logistic support base for Swift Boats and LSTs off the coast. At Cat Lo I trained to operate landing craft (LCM 3,6,8), drive a 60-ton crawler crane, operate a Rough Terrain forklift, splice wire, pour wire sockets, and splice nylon lines. But most important, I learned how to work with and teach young Vietnamese sailors those same skills.

It was then I first recognized my ability to effectively communicate and instruct young people. I developed a rapport and became excited each day to work as well as learn in their company. **DPL number 3: By learning all the skills required of an assigned position, a leader may gain the respect of his subordinates.**

The importance of learning how to communicate and encouraging subordinates to come to you with questions or problems became obvious to me after a painful encounter with my best Vietnamese friend. I was attempting to teach a young petty officer, Nguyen Cao Thung, how to operate an 83-foot landing craft. The currents in the rivers in Nam are strong and quick and maneuvering a large boat is an acquired skill. I became frustrated and used some derogatory language toward the young sailor, accusing him of being not too bright. He turned to me and said, "I speak Vietnamese, English, French, and Chinese. How about you?"

Other than the fact that he made a great point, something else occurred to me: Whatever possessed me to hurt a friend or risk a relationship over something so trivial? **DPL number 4: Always use respectful language when dealing with people; never purposely be demeaning or hurtful. If you slip, apologize—sincerely.**

Leadership lessons I learned in Vietnam (and later in my military life) are equally applicable in a public school setting.

Take DPL4, for instance. Nothing is more inappropriate than using demeaning or hurtful language to a student. I remember when I was assigned to a high school with a reputation of being undisciplined and poorly led, with poor test scores. Attendance by students and staff was abysmal. Leadership and staff never talked positively about students. In short, it was a place nobody wished to be assigned.

I avoided the teachers' lounge to be away from the negativity. As much as I attempted to share skills that I knew worked well with young people, I was just "the military guy." What did I know about education?

Well, this old military guy knew if students were happy and treated with a modicum of respect and they enjoyed your class, learning was going to naturally follow. In the five years I worked at the school I never wrote up a student for discipline, never had an argument or raised my voice with a student, my students had an almost perfect attendance rate, and their test scores went up.

I would stand cafeteria duty and at the end of lunch students would be high-fiving me as they left, while the other teacher

5

who was on duty with me (a real jerk) would leave looking like he had just been engaged in the famous Animal House food fight.

Now, you may think that I must be easy on students, especially for a Navy guy. Far from it. Did I mention that I served a tour of duty as a Company Commander (Navy equivalent to a drill Instructor)? Believe me, that takes a firm hand. The fact of the matter is I loved and respected all my students, the same as I did my sailors.

So, when I moved on to education, I took with me the lessons I had learned in a 25-year Navy career. The remaining chapters of this book will address the connectivity of Deckplate Leadership, education, resource gathering and community engagement.

CHAPTER 2

Good Shoes

*His cardinal mistake is that he isolates himself,
and allows nobody to see him; and by which he
does not know what is going on in the very matter
he is dealing with.*

*-- Abraham Lincoln, regarding his relieving
Gen. John C. Fremont of his command,
September 9,1861*

I believe one of the best tidbits of advice I ever offered to young petty officers as well as prospective teachers, principals, and future leaders is that all great Deckplate Leaders have at least two things in common: energy and comfortable shoes.

Management By Walking Around (MBWA) is a tool that has been discussed and used in the corporate world for years. It means you must get up from your desk and be seen in order to gain knowledge of your business.

On a nuclear aircraft carrier with a crew of more than 5,500, it is vital that those executing orders know and trust the person issuing the commands. When I reported aboard the USS Dwight D. Eisenhower I made it my top priority that the crew would learn my name, leadership style, military reputation, sense of humor, and my idiosyncrasies in record time. I made it part of my day to stand at the gangplank in port when the crew came aboard in the morning and when they departed in the evening, greeting each sailor. I produced a TV show once or twice a week and had it shown during meal hours and in the evening. I provided information to the crew regarding schedules, training, discipline, and commanding officer memos, as well as some well-placed rumors and good fun. My photo graced the Plan of the Day and our weekly *Ike Bulletin* newspaper. I had an article in each publication and each day I attended morning quarters of one of the numerous divisions. In the evenings, I wandered through the various spaces and made a point of stopping and talking with sailors of all ranks. I would play a game of cards, answer questions, or tell a joke or two. The Captain and I also visited spaces together and at times manned the serving line in the crew's mess, which the sailors got a kick out of.

The result of all this is that you would be hard pressed to find an Ike sailor who did not know his Command Master Chief or one who would be intimidated or shy about approaching me with a concern. My relationship with the crew was based on honesty and respect and I had little difficulty sharing with them both the good and the bad. My requests were typically met with an "aye aye."

Getting to know you

I took this attitude to my first school, where I was surprised by the number of students who had no idea of the name of their principal. Some said they only saw their school leader at assemblies and most had never spoken with him, unless they had the misfortune of being sent to the office. Not unexpectedly, I discovered weak leadership and low morale at the school. I returned to my old ways and was all over the school and in no time was noticed by the superintendent, who told me I should consider going into administration. No thanks, I was having too much fun working with the students. In a school of 1,000, they all knew I was the Navy Junior Reserve Officer Training Corps instructor and, just as on the carrier, positive relations were resulting in a well-disciplined environment. As an associate Naval Science instructor, I observed how much the cadets appreciated attention. Just as a word from superiors to sailors was welcome, it was even more appreciated by the young men and women in the corps of cadets. It meant a great deal to them to see me at their sport practices, academic events, after-school clubs, and other activities. This extra attention and support from me caused the cadets to respond in a positive manner, and I even received emails from parents telling me how much their children enjoyed JROTC.

Fast forward

Years later, when I decided to build and lead my own school as Commandant of the Delaware Military Academy, I vowed to ensure that all students knew me by the end of the first week. I initiated a weekly bulletin, *Commandant's Comments*, ate in the mess hall with the cadets, stayed in the halls during class changes, hosted special lunches with cadets in my conference room, and went room to room in the morning greeting cadets. One action was especially effective and became a tradition: The Commandant Rocking Chair.

Each morning a cadet was assigned to bring out to the school bus stop the Commandant's rocking chair. It was decorated with a Navy and Marine Corps flag, was inscribed "Commandant," and came with a warm military blanket for cold mornings. Arriving school buses would pull up to the chair and as cadets debarked they would salute and I would return the gesture. This accomplished four things: 1) They immediately knew they were at school and should head to homeroom. 2) I had an opportunity to look at their uniform and make remarks like "looks like you shined your shoes with a Hershey bar today" or "you look awesome." 3) I was able to read their name tag. And, most important, number 4—making eye contact and hearing their good morning. If "good morning" seemed a little off or sad, I would ask to see them after homeroom. On more than one occasion this gave me an opportunity to put out a fire and help the student make his or her day a little brighter. Sitting in the chair while it snowed as parents drove by waving and honking was a bonus.

I came to be identified with the chair. During Army/Navy week I arrived at school one day to find my chair had been run up the flagpole. I thought it was a clever prank and was honored to have a relationship where cadets felt comfortable enough in knowing it would be good for a laugh. Another time, after I attended an education conference for two days, I received calls and emails regarding my health since I was not at my usual post, my chair. After that, the cadets and I decided in order to alarm no one about my health we would have the chair in place each morning regardless of my presence. As a leader of a school, nothing is better than the love of your students and the respect of your parents and staff, and that chair proved to me that I had both.

I made myself available at all times. I never had a problem getting up from a meeting during class changes and stepping into the hall to be with students. I never scheduled meetings during lunch. Making sure that your boss as well as your staff know that interaction with students is a priority is important. Superintendents who call principals' meetings during the school day or board members making impromptu visits should know how you stand; do not waiver. Imagine if you were absent the day the worst happened. Superintendents and board members are not responsible for student safety, you are. At the end of the day when all is quiet, you may return to your office and attend to administrative duties. (It's also not a bad time to remove your shoes and rub those sore feet.)

CHAPTER 3

········●·●·●·······

Leadership Climate and Culture

It is the art of the supreme teacher to awaken joy in creative expression and knowledge.

Albert Einstein

There are many indicators of a successful school. Among them are a strong curriculum, student achievements, outstanding instructional delivery, proper financing and resources, and parent support. However, having founded and led two successful schools, I believe the most important factor is a strong, positive school culture.

The culture and climate come from the top. As a teacher/ principal or a military NCO, you must be able to read the climate, identify problems and propose and apply corrective measures. By doing so, you may have students and faculty racing to school in the morning and leaving reluctantly at night, having truly found a wonderful learning environment. I have been in such a school—where students complained about winter break being too long and wondered why we didn't have activities in the summer.

There are many schools like this, but you don't hear about them. Public schools are notorious for failing to market themselves by touting these qualities. For many years, there was no need for them to do this, because there was no competition for students. Times are changing, and with the proliferation of charter schools, all schools are now competing for enrollment. Schools that are safe and offer strong academics and a positive culture are going to win, because it comes down to survival of the fittest. And those that are proficient at telling their success stories will have the edge.

Starting at the top

Recently I visited schools where negativity, zero tolerance discipline policies, micro management of teachers, little or no school spirit and low faculty and student morale were evident everywhere. I came to these schools supposedly at the request of the school leader to see if I might offer recommendations on school improvement. I quickly sensed the invitation came from someone other than the principal because no one displayed any interest in my arrival, and my observations and suggestions received meaningless nods of acknowledgement. To the chagrin of the State Association of School Administrators, however, I reported to the superintendent that "these schools do indeed have a path to significant improvement: Get rid of the principals! Re-assign them to intensive leadership training and if evaluated as showing no noticeable positive change in behaviors after completion of the training, remove their certification."

I am always amazed at the lack of emphasis placed on leadership training when filling such an important position as the principal, someone who is responsible for preparing young women and men for life. In the Navy, we have commanding officers with more than 20 years of leadership experience assigned to ships and bases. Prior to assuming command, however, they are required to attend five to six months of Commanding Officer school and receive specialized training, including leadership. And they are held to high standards. The *Navy Times* of March 10, 2016 reported that 18 commanding officers had been fired the previous year for poor decision making, a function of leadership.

I am sure firings occur in the education sector. However, I must live in an area where exceptional leadership skills are the norm. In 25 years, I've only heard of a few who lost positions due to poor leadership; certainly not 18 in one year. Perhaps it happens more frequently, but it is not publicly reported since it is a personnel matter.

Rewards

Including students and staff in decision making as well as acknowledging them for a job well done are crucial steps in establishing a positive command climate and school culture. Any leader worth his salt has ongoing programs of recognition and reward.

In the Navy, when we were off on deployment it was imperative to focus on crew morale. It was relatively easy to come up with rewards for outstanding performance, given the resources available on a nuclear aircraft carrier. For those crew members who spent hours down in the hot engineering spaces, a few hours up on the flight deck, a ride in a helo, or a simple break from routine were welcome. If you are in a management position, always be on the lookout for opportunities to provide a form of appreciation for the work of the personnel in your charge.

As a principal, you can hold a luncheon once a month for outstanding students. They receive recognition and you receive valuable feedback on school climate. On the last period of the day on Friday, take over a teacher's class so that he or she may leave early. Have your assistant principal do the same, and keep a record to ensure all faculty are included. Teachers love it, and when it comes time to ask for additional help with a project, they will line up to volunteer.

Be innovative, exciting, and daring in your reward system. Go above and beyond. Spend time figuring out how to be positive and do good things for staff and students. Rides in helos is out for students, but a head-of-the line pass for lunch or an early dismissal are unexpected rewards and highly valued. Contacting parents of students to laud their performance and tell them how highly they are prized as students will go far. Military personnel, teachers, students, and parents enjoy receiving praise and recognition. Utilize this asset you possess and which you employed throughout your tour in the military.

Collaboration with staff

Many of you have heard repeatedly that the school principal is the instructional leader of the school. To me that sounds somewhat presumptuous. That's not me by a long shot. Understanding and determining good instruction comes with the job. I prefer to consider myself simply a leader. Teachers have degrees in their subject areas and have been trained in pedagogy. There are seasoned department chairs as direct supervisors and they are accountable to the administration. Data important to the mission of the school is shared and work is conducted collaboratively to employ measures for best chances of success. When a decision is to be made at school, unless it involves safety and security, the adage of two heads are better than one usually holds true.

As a new teacher, you may run into those who, when presented with an idea or proposal, immediately respond,

"Oh, we tried that and it doesn't work." Sound familiar? I know you have heard that in the military. Just as in the service, the educators who oppose your suggestions are often those responsible for the project failure. When you report to a new command, avoid the naysayers like the plague. And as a new teacher you should do the same.

Time for a sea story. On deployment to the Persian Gulf aboard the IKE we were looking for activities that would have a positive impact on crew morale. I approached our captain with the "Home for Dinner Program." This is where American families living in the ports we would be visiting would host sailors for dinner. The Captain said he had participated in these programs before and they were normally not well received by the crew, and few attended. Remember, I mentioned what a great skipper we had? Well, he authorized us to run with it because he thought previous attempts suffered from lackluster leadership and he was anxious to see if we could make it work. Our chaplain and his assistants were a dynamic group, and they volunteered to oversee the program. The senior NCO community were onboard with the idea and through the efforts of these amazing sailors, hundreds of our crewmembers had enjoyable evenings, made great friends, and ate well. So much for the "it will never work" crew. Solid leadership and hard work always come through.

Collaboration and communication with staff up and down the chain of command works in a school just as it does in a military organization. Teachers, aides, cafeteria workers, custodial staff, bus drivers, crossing guards, coaches, nurses, and administrative staff are the lifeblood of your school. (Later, I will discuss in more detail the group that plays a vital role in the development of the school culture and climate: students.)

When you have the opportunity, I recommend that you go on the internet and find the article "Message to Garcia," by Elbert Hubbard. Read it several times. The more you dig into this simple three-page article about a young lieutenant, the more the concept of Deckplate Leadership will become clear.

First impressions

In the Navy when you report aboard a ship you step into an area known as the quarterdeck, where you are greeted by the Petty Officer of the Watch. You have an immediate indication of the professionalism of the command by the neatness, organization, and cleanliness of the area. The same holds true for a school. A front office that is cluttered and confusing versus one that is neat, orderly and exuding a cheerful "how may I help you" atmosphere speaks well of the school's professionalism.

We feel more comfortable at the doctor, dentist, law office, and bank when an air of professionalism prevails. These are all places where you conduct important business about your health, finances, and legal matters. Shouldn't the venue for *the* most important business in your life— the education of your child—be equally if not more professional? The receptionist at your school, the cafeteria workers, custodians, transportation drivers, nurses, coaches, and counselors are on the front line representing your organization. Their value cannot be overstated. Even substitute teachers should be familiar with your standards and behavior expectations. Anyone representing your organization is responsible for how you are presented to your clients.

Greetings to staff and cadets/students

I was hired as an Associate Navy Junior Reserve Officer Training Corps instructor at a school in Seaford, Delaware, in August 1993. In the first few days of observation it was evident I was working in an environment of high negativity. One particular issue occurred each morning as the students arrived. Our school board had mandated that hats were not to be worn in the building. When students arrived, they were greeted by a chorus of "take your hat off or you will be written up" instead of "good morning." I went to the principal and asked if we could allow students to wear their hats into the school and ask them to remove them when they enter the classroom. He said he was willing to try, but needed to have the board's approval. Fortunately, they agreed to test the idea. The students thought it was a good plan and we initiated the new policy the first school day of the following week. "Good morning" changed the entire dynamic of the school. Teachers and students were greeting each other with a smile, high fives, and fist bumps. Starting the day on a positive note was great for all.

Another policy required students to have hall passes during class time. We had hall monitors assigned to locations throughout the school whose responsibility was to make sure students had authorized passes. However, it seemed that all staff members were asking students to show their passes to the point that they felt teachers assumed they were up to something nefarious. I am all about safety and security, but I want students to feel comfortable when they see me in the hall—not immediately challenged. Unless you are suspicious of some wrongdoing, let others do their job, give the student a positive greeting, and assume he or she is on an authorized pass.

As a teacher, role model, and adult in your student's life, failing to return a greeting can be devastating to students, who are at a sensitive stage of their young lives. If they acknowledge you, it means they care. So, any time you have an opportunity to respond kindly to a student, do so. It's the right thing to do – always.

Students: your right arm

Successful schools are identified by the academic and behavioral performance of their students. As an administrator, you should make sure that the student government or student council has input about major decisions on school behavior codes. You may be surprised to find they are sometimes stricter than adults. Meet with class leaders periodically and encourage participation. A school with engaged students in all aspects of student life is a winner. Schools who ignore this amazing human resource are really missing out.

As a teacher, it's important to receive your own report card, not from your boss but from your employees—your class. As you develop rapport with your students, they will become more honest with you, sometimes brutally so. Take their critiques seriously. And as you implement corrective action, acknowledge and respond to their input. There may be instances in their evaluation of you where they may not fully grasp why you have certain behaviors, and an explanation may go a long way. Know that whatever positive action you take will help you grow in their eyes, and be assured the word will spread throughout the school about your fairness and trustworthiness.

I have found that as students mature you need to make adjustments in your relationships. Gradually up the ante and treat them in a more adult manner. Discipline is a great example. When a freshman makes a mistake, you need to be strict to ensure there will be a behavior modification. When a senior makes a mistake, being strict is not especially effective, but expressing disappointment in their behavior may work well.

Engaging kids in the way their school operates and treating them with respect creates an environment that they want to be part of. I was once asked what data I relied on to identify an effective, well-run school. My response was immediate: the daily attendance report. High attendance indicates that students enjoy coming to school and will typically have low behavioral incidents. You can't educate kids until they are in the building and in their seats.

CHAPTER 4

· · · · · ·•••••● ●•••••· · · · ·

Show Me The Money!

The only mistake you can make is not asking for help.

Cardiologist and Author Dr. Sandeep Jauhar

The task of raising money for schools has changed since the economic turmoil of 2008. Grant money is being awarded, but nowhere near the amounts of previous levels. While charitable foundations and philanthropists are still in abundance and continue to give, they are more careful about how their dollars are distributed, ensuring that their money is well placed to accomplish the most good. Institutions and teachers requesting funds must provide detailed data, projected outcomes, and plans for community engagement. Competition is stiff, but if you do your homework and prepare your request properly, your chances of a positive response are excellent.

Over the past 20 years, I have secured funding for several projects and the construction of two schools. While I have had a few rejections, I have found the best route to success is a transparent explanation of how money is to be used. Otherwise, your proposal will not even be considered. In fact, before you submit a request for a grant, exhaust all other avenues and have solid documentation as evidence of those attempts.

I do not wish to go over all the negatives of education funding, or lack of, save one, and that is the government. Allow me to attempt a nautical analogy. Suppose your ship is sinking due to a collision with a floating object. You have four holes in the hull and need to plug them to save the ship. You report to damage control central (emergency operations) and request four plug kits but are informed that you will have to do your best with three because, due to a cost cutting measure, the normal supply of 10 kits per ship has been slashed to three and if you wish to stay afloat you will have to be innovative. Similarly, it seems every year our state budget is in trouble and we must tighten our belts and everyone must make sacrifices. In other words, there aren't enough plugs for all the holes in our schools.

Government normally escapes the budget axe. Recently, at a ceremony for veterans, another group always at the forefront fighting to save what was promised to them for their service, the audience was asked to applaud two legislators who each had served 40 years in the State Legislature. Here are legislators who for four decades worked in an organization that has incurred huge debt, while education goes begging. Yet they were being honored!

Many state finances are an absolute mess and although I don't doubt that legislators try, they—and we—must do better. The answer to every one of the world's problems is education. *Everything* needs to be cut, including government, before one dime of education funds is touched. An educated society is a great society and has the intelligence to tackle tough situations.

Unfortunately, convincing a state government that awards gold watches for length of service that education is our top priority is probably a losing battle. The days of raising taxes in referendums for public schools are numbered. The anti-charter movement is well funded and will continue to block access to capital funds, depriving 10 percent of our kids adequate facilities. Meanwhile, private and parochial schools are becoming out of reach for most students due to rising tuition costs. While this sounds grim, there is hope.

Public charter school vs. traditional public school

In the early 1990s the charter movement began in Minnesota, and it changed the face of traditional public education. Charters are independent public schools operating under an atmosphere of relaxed bureaucracy so it may be easier to implement different approaches to education and, if successful, share those approaches with their public school partners. For example, charters in some states are allowed to offer preferences, such as accepting only students who have demonstrated an interest in the charter's designated mission and who live within a certain radius of the school. Charters may also have the authority to ask a student not to return the following year if the student has shown a lack of interest in the school's mission.

In many states, charters are not authorized capital funding and are required to raise funds for their facilities. The anti-charter movement made sure of this provision, hoping it would guarantee failure. You might think any attempt to improve upon the current educational system would be embraced and nurtured. So why is there an anti-charter movement? One reason is that charter school teachers are on one-year contracts and basically must perform to serve, which is a basic tenet in the business world. However, in education there is teacher tenure, which in many cases is granted after three years and assures continued employment. Also, unlike public school teachers, charter teachers are non-union and do not pay dues.

The anti-charter movement claims that charters hand

pick their students, which is false. Attorneys General review acceptance policies to make sure they are in accordance with state code. Discipline rules, state testing, administrative reporting requirements, and IDEA compliance are all required. There are now more than 7,000 charter schools serving three million students. If a charter does not meet the defined objectives, it must surrender its charter. If a traditional public school fails, the answer has been to throw more money at the problem. The unfortunate rift between the two entities is sad.

If you are making the move to education, you need to understand the difference between charter and public schools. Charter employees are state employees but in many cases are paid at a lower scale as a result of the loss of capital funding. All other state benefits are unaffected. The one big hammer that charter has is that a problem student may be asked not to return. As a result, you have a school with students who have asked to attend and are willing to play by the established rules.

There is a valid reason why charters do not receive capital funding. Imagine if the taxpayers funded the building of a school that failed in year two. The state would be saddled with an empty building. Makes good business sense. What does not make sense, however, is the answer—or rather, non-answer—I get when I ask a legislator or Education Secretary the following question: When a charter school has been renewed after its initial charter, typically five years, has an established waiting list, met all the charter's objectives, has been renewed, Middle States certified, has passed all financial audits, and has exceeded state standards on mandated testing, why should it continue to be deprived of capital funding? That question is typically answered with a blank stare.

A major objection you often hear is that charter schools are draining off all the good kids (tuition money). I find that statement objectionable. Anyone who does not consider all kids the best kids should not be allowed to work in education.

However, charter schools *are* taking the best parents because they are highly involved in their children's education.

When I was a principal of a traditional public school with 1,100 students, I would hold the PTA meeting in my office. Typically, the president, vice president, treasurer, and secretary would attend. That is not to say all PTAs behave in a similar fashion; I'm sure there are many examples of highly productive, traditional organizations. However, at my last charter school of 1,000 students, I had to hold PTA meetings in the auditorium and people would be standing in the back of the room. Quite a contrast, and evidence that charters are winning the recruiting war.

Traditional public schools and opponents of charters claim the loss of students' tuition funding is devastating to public education. However, the argument they do not want to hear is this: While they lose 10 students and their tuition funding, they are allowed to keep the capital funding for the students they are not required to serve. *Hmmm!*

There's a simple answer to competition: Offer a better product. That may also fall under the heading "adapt and overcome." This may seem odd coming from a charter school founder, but the best thing that could ever happen to education would be that all charter schools close down due to lack of enrollment. In other words, public schools would be forced to perform at such a high level that there would be no need for charters.

Those opposing the charter movement may want to come to the realization that it is here to stay, and perhaps they should consider working with charter leaders to make all schools successful. There is power in unity.

There is a path forward for both
charters and traditional schools

There is a way to move forward and make our school system number one in the world. I have been working at it since 2003. I resigned from the "oh, woe is me crowd," ignoring all the cost-cutters, and raised money on my own. I have become proficient at this and if schools are to keep pace and continue to advance, their principals will have to do the same and become resource providers and CEOs. School boards, many of which believe their role is to micro-manage principals, are going to have to deliver resources just as a corporate board is required to do to keep a company solvent.

Bake sales, manning the concession stands, selling poinsettias, frozen pizzas, silent auctions, golf tournaments, band boosters, athletic boosters, school pride clothing, and pancake breakfasts are fun, although they're all time consuming. They are okay for funding some school activities and a local field trip or two, but not for funding technology upgrades, new athletic fields, capital projects, overseas travel, and other high ticket items. Those require grants, capital campaigns, and generous donors. Colleges and universities have strong alumni for financial support. That is usually not the case at the high school level.

So where do you start?

First of all, your story is all-important. For years, our school system, at least in the public sector, has not had to worry about competing for enrollment. The numbers and the feeder patterns were established and budgets were relatively reliable. Meanwhile, private and parochial schools have been telling their story and competing for years while relying heavily upon alumni families for students and financial support.

Our local newspaper runs a section once a week that is dedicated to high schools. Schools submit articles about events and activities and major achievements. This is at no cost. Public schools with more than 1,000 students often do not submit articles, or submit only a sentence or two. It's hard to believe schools with such large enrollments have nothing positive to report.

Many middle schools hold high school nights in the fall. This offers an opportunity for the 7th and 8th grade classes to visit with counselors from local schools and obtain information to assist them in selecting a high school. Typically, all charter schools are present as well as parochial and independent schools. Seldom are the public schools represented. As a school leader, you need to attend these events and present an honest and truthful story about your school.

The advent of charter schools has created a paradigm shift. Some charter schools fail and close down. Rightfully so—either perform or don't waste taxpayer money. However, those charters that are performing are offering an outstanding product at no cost. This causes a void in the traditional public school and has hit the parochial schools equally hard. So now all schools are recruiting. And since the number of school seats available is greater than eligible students, some schools will lose this competition. So, whoever has the best story to tell, backed by solid data and coupled with enticing economic factors, is going to thrive.

My experience with many public high schools is that they have some wonderful activities and programs but are weak in how they convey that information to the community. One PR director informed me they do very well distributing district bulletins by direct mail and on their website. Well, few read the mail nowadays and if you do not have a child in one of their schools, why would you go to their website? Several large districts I visited have had the same person in charge of public relations for more than 20 years. There is nothing wrong with experience -- unless you don't adapt and change with the times.

Create and develop your story. You should have several.

One of some length for discussion with members of the community and one short elevator story (two minutes). Identify who you wish to hear the story.

Education in many locations has ignored its greatest potential partner and resource provider: *the business community.* If I were a young man and could get back into the school principal business, my first stop would be at my State Chamber of Commerce. They get it!

Partner with your state, city, and county Chambers of Commerce. Get them into your school, have the students tell the story of your programs, activities and plans. Ask for their advice and, more important, heed that advice.

As Commandant of the military academy I would host a formal lunch at school once a month for eight students and two members of the business community. We had fine china and silver donated to us by a local club, and would set a beautiful table. Our parents' organization would prepare a gourmet lunch. I made sure students were not invited more than once so that as many as possible attended a luncheon. It became quite an honor. Before attending one, students received a class in etiquette and were required to RSVP. They were also schooled in what was and was not appropriate for discussion at a business luncheon and were told to dress for success. We did this to tell our story and to show off our wonderful students.

I tear up when thinking about the magnitude of support the business community has provided our schools as a result of these events. We have been the recipients of grants, internships, in-kind services, recommendations, guest teaching, and Principal for a Day events. Many in the business community have become friends, ready to respond to any request.

In the Navy/military we are all too familiar with the budget axe and have become masters of swapping supplies and gathering resources. Veterans have an edge when it comes to asking for help, having been on the short end for quite some time. Accomplishing the impossible with little is a way of life in our military, unfortunately.

No money? No problem

Co- founding the Delaware Military Academy, an all-Navy, tuition-free, JROTC High School, cost $12 million. We convinced a local contractor to build the school based upon the story we presented: it would be the first of its kind in the U.S. We had the support of the Navy, local and federal officials, a charter granted by the local district, and a vision and passion to make it a reality. The contractor agreed and built the school knowing we had no money until we had students in the seats. He believed in our vision and was behind us all the way.

Selling the idea of entrusting their most precious commodity, their children, into our hands when we did not even have a building was more than a leap of faith for parents. We shared the vision with the community. We held town hall meetings, did radio interviews, made presentations at school board meetings, published newspaper and magazine articles, attended school nights at local schools, and stood outside grocery stores with flyers. Any time we could put our name in a positive light we took advantage. Sharing our story, along with our professional reputations and the NAVY JROTC record for excellence in training, helped us recruit 300 students for the opening year. Our motto was "To Get Famous Fast."

The greatest danger we faced was not recruiting, funding, instruction, or staffing. It was the fear of failing to deliver on the promised mission and cheating students out of a high school experience. You cannot tell parents and students that because you are a new school they need to be patient before we can have Friday night football, dances, school rings, yearbooks, and all the amenities of student life. Students currently in school are not interested in a new field house to be built five years after they are gone. As Commandant, my number one priority was to make sure cadets were not short-changed on any aspect of student life and to convince them they would have fun working to establish those activities. Homecoming would happen.

All these activities require funding and the local community rallied, resulting in the following:

1. A tile company provided $60,000 in tile they had stored as excess.
2. A quarry had a $10,000 8X10 piece of black marble that had been erroneously cut. They engraved the school name on it and installed it at the front entrance.
3. The Navy provided a ship's bell and two large anchors for the front of the school. They also pay half the salaries of the seven Naval Instructors and provide more than $500,000 in uniforms for the students.
4. A gym donated all the weights for our weight room.
5. A phone company paid for installation of high-speed internet and 60 laptops.
6. A veterans group provided a Civil War cannon and a WWII mural for our mess hall.
7. The PTA purchased an ice machine, warming ovens and a snow plow.
8. A florist provides prom flowers and graduation flowers.
9. A local car dealership provided a driver's ed car free of charge.
10. The Navy Fleet Reserve Association purchased a $25,000 weather station.
11. U.S. Lacrosse provided $25,000 in lacrosse equipment.
12. A local business donated 25 teachers' desks, chalkboards, teachers' chairs, and marker boards.
13. A clothing company provided clothing racks for military uniforms.
14. Local veterans groups donated flags for school decoration.

15. The Navy provided historical paintings for wall decoration.
16. The first year we were open local police provided coverage for dances and events at no charge.
17. The Longwood, Welfare, Carpenter, Laffey McHugh and Elise MacDonald Foundations donated a total of $1.2 million.
18. County government donated $25,000.
19. Parents and friends purchased $250,000 in commemorative bricks for our front entrance.
20. Veterans groups and individuals donated $75,000.

I think you have the idea: the community was engaged. The most important lesson here is that major donors like foundations and philanthropists are more apt to support your organization when many players have demonstrated their trust through investment.

No tax dollars went into the construction of the school. And it continues to grow. Now in its 13th year, DMA has more than 550 cadets and a long waiting list for acceptance. It is guided by strong leadership and an active corporate board. The community support is amazing, continuing to provide funding and in-kind services.

Another small example of the engagement at DMA: A cadet slipped and fell one day and put his elbow through the drywall. Having no money to repair the hole, I sent out a plea to parents, asking if they knew anyone who could fix the wall for no cost. Within an hour, four contractors arrived to repair the damage. Gosh, I loved that school!

If you are contemplating building and opening a charter school, that subject will be discussed in detail later in the book. You may wish to take advantage of my contact information and speak one-on-one with me about the experience—pro bono, of course. By the way, pro bono is popular and welcome in the charter community.

The USEED adventure

On to something new: project based fundraising. Several months ago, I was speaking with the commandant of a new military academy, First State Military Academy, located in Clayton, Delaware. He was lamenting the fact that he would not be able to provide the physical resources for his students that he had promised due to lack of funding and support. I asked him for specifics and he identified the immediate need for a professional Marine Corps obstacle course. The cost would be $25,000. This was just one of many projects in the queue at that price range. As one with experience in raising funds and now a full-time advisor (old guy with little to do), I asked him to let me look into one project at a time to see what we might accomplish. I had heard of GoFundme and CrowdFunding as excellent ways to raise money. After researching those sources, however, I discovered they had only a 10 percent success rate.

I then was referred to USEED, a fundraising business sponsoring project based learning (PBL) that had been created at the University of Delaware and is currently located at Arizona State University. USEED offered online funding specifically for PBL at the university level. As luck would have it, I was acquainted with one of their board members and I asked him if he felt this platform could be adapted for a project like ours at a charter high school. I examined how they ran a 30-day funding campaign and discovered it was easily adaptable. We asked if they would consider allowing us to pilot a test program. An attractive feature was to allow the 9.9 percent administrative fee to be added onto the project goal. Charter schools have no up-front funds to authorize and would be responsible only for the percentage of funds raised up to the campaign goal. So, our $25,000 goal would cost $2475. They agreed and we established our goal at $27,500 to pay for the project and the administrative fees. We launched our web page with our appeal, the most important component being a video created by two students that outlined our project and emphasized the need. It was reviewed by USEED, and after we made several changes based on their recommendations, we were ready to go.

Although technologically challenged, I wanted to be the person to run the test and input the data to determine if it was an efficient way for a principal to rapidly initiate a project funding campaign, allowing a project to proceed without having to wait for a grant submission date or a school board approval. What made this different from other crowdfunding sites was that there was ongoing training, email prompts and templates, chat support, and an incredibly easy platform to navigate.

As the program manager, I was required to recruit 20 team members, faculty, friends, parents and students. I did so, and then we attended a 45-minute online training demonstration and orientation. Each member had to provide a list of 20 people who they thought might donate to our campaign or at least help spread the word. The launch date to send out our appeal was set, and a template for a well-constructed appeal letter.

A feature of the USEED platform is that you have the capability to utilize parts of the email templates and personalize the rest, which is strongly recommended to achieve success. We established four levels of giving, along with small incentives. We emphasized participation and not the amount of the gift.

Two days after launch we had raised $4000. The platform allows you to immediately thank donors and to track the numbers of participants. By the end of week one we had 50 percent of our goal; after two weeks we had 95 percent, and by the end of week three we were at 105 percent. We closed our campaign with 121 percent of goal, or $33,310. Construction began in March of 2017, and the obstacle course was completed in two months. USEED has agreed to continue the pilot program for several more campaigns in traditional public schools, charter schools, and private and parochial schools.

Now for the real bombshell and added value of the

USEED project: 170 participants, businesses, parents, local officials, veterans organizations, students, a chief of police, and construction companies donated $6000 of material and labor. In addition, the National Guard, Army Reserve, and numerous factions of the community played major roles in the campaigns success. It is the only professional obstacle course in the state of Delaware and will host events and be available to first responders, military organizations and other schools with JROTC and ROTC units.

In the small town of Clayton, because of the USEED experience, a new level of philanthropy has been created. Regardless of an individual's economic situation, this type of crowdfunding allows everyone to participate and become part of the project's success. I am very happy for the First State Military Academy, their Corps of Cadets, and *Bravo Zulu!* (Navy speak for well done) to all the donors.

CHAPTER 5

· · · · · ·●●●●●●●● · · · · · · · · · ·

Military Leader to School Teacher

I, Charles William Baldwin, do solemnly swear to support and defend the Constitution of the United States against all enemies, foreign and domestic; that I will bear truth, faith and allegiance to the same and that I will obey the orders of the President of the United States and the orders of those appointed over me according to regulations and the Uniform Code of Military Justice, so help me God.

We begin our military service with the Oath of Enlistment – powerful words that set a standard of performance in our daily routines and, for those who choose to make a career in the military, throughout their lives. It often crosses my mind how so many in the civilian world would find taking such an oath objectionable in their current positions. Imagine working for an organization requiring you to *obey* your managers and pledge *allegiance* to said organization. I'm not sure if I know of any labor unions that would buy into that regulation. That said, responding to the requests of management and a sense of loyalty to your employer are good things and should be expected of good employees.

In our public school system, disdain for regulations, students, parents, and the administration must be eradicated. You will do well to remember your military oath and let it guide you in the field of education. Loyalty and a great work ethic are highly valued and usually rewarded.

Being assigned to the USS Dwight D. Eisenhower (IKE) as Command Master Chief was a high point in my Navy career. The responsibility of working with more than 5500 crew and Air Wing personnel was the ultimate test of my leadership ability. It prepared me to enter the field of education with confidence. Upon retirement from active service the preparation and foundation to engage and lead others had been well established. It included time management, organizational skills, discipline (of self and others), communication skills (oral and written), respect for authority as well as peers and subordinates, work ethic, leading by example, punctuality, grooming standards, sense of appropriate humor, and physical fitness. The trait or ability that stands out, though, is setting standards and holding sailors or students accountable to those standards.

My commanding officer on IKE, Rear Admiral William Cross, is an outstanding leader, mentor, and friend. He would reinforce the critical importance of the command, establishing expectations and standards and ensuring sailors adhered to policy and performed at or above (normally above) acceptable levels. Thanks to his leadership style, the crew held him in high regard and to a man assumed his peers were probably all playing catch up. The rewards of his policies were incredible, most notably when we completed a six-month deployment to the Persian Gulf and Arctic Circle and returned home after 9500 launches and landings with all our aircraft intact and, more important, all our sailors, safe and sound, returning to their families.

When I retired from IKE and went into education I placed above my desk a sign that read, "You are either getting better or getting worse"—a statement the admiral was fond of sharing with me and I in turn with the crew and my students. Do not accept the status quo. Take steps to improve yourself.

The consequences of failing to adhere to standards was demonstrated during the Vietnam War. The U.S. Navy was under the command of Admiral Elmo Zumwalt, a great patriot, American, and naval officer. He became noted for his directives, known as Z-grams, which were attempts to modernize our personnel policies and regulations. He was a forward thinker, but many of his subordinates did not agree with his initiatives and felt as if he was allowing the fad of the day or the troops to establish regulations based upon their preference. Instead of embracing their leader's ideas, some subordinates half-heartedly implemented them and the resulting turmoil doomed them to be reversed and resulted in a return to the status quo. It took the Navy several years to recover from the fast pace of change and many important lessons regarding implementing change were learned. Even the best ideas require collaboration and acceptance by all, regardless of whether it affects them directly.

Class size

As a new teacher, you will hear repeatedly, beginning with the first day of school, about class size. The cry of "how do you expect me to teach so many students effectively?" is heard in teachers lounges all over the country. School boards and parents are outraged over class size. Politicians run for office with the promise of reducing class size. I suspect if you went to an Italian school the first day of the new academic year you would hear, "Mama Mia, quanti ragazzi!" (My mother, how many kids!).

Allow me to go over this carefully. If you have 10 students sitting quietly at their desks listening to you and taking notes and asking good questions, would you say this was a fair class size? What about 11 students exhibiting the same behavior? 12?13?14? When is it too many? How about 30 sitting quietly? The answer is it is not about class size, it is about classroom discipline and management.

When I was a Company Commander in basic training, I had 84 recruits in my company. I taught them every day, all day, and never had an issue. That's why I can't buy the class size argument. If I have 34 desks in my classroom, then I expect 34 students.

When I was studying for my certification as a high school principal, my professor shared a wonderful story about class size. He was a former principal and not sympathetic to the class size argument. When approached by a group of teachers whining about class sizes, he responded, "Jesus Christ was the greatest teacher that ever lived. He only had 12 students and one of them went bad. Now leave me alone."

Well said.

Discipline

Lessons in discipline give the military veteran a distinct advantage in the classroom compared to the rookie teacher fresh out of college. I recall as a principal hiring a young man who had recently completed his enlistment in the Marines. As a Navy man, I have deep admiration and respect for Marines. Our country is so fortunate to have them on the front lines and I can't recall ever meeting a bad Marine. He came aboard as School Resource Officer in charge of discipline. Students were immediately impressed by his outstanding physical condition and presence. His most admirable attribute, however, was how well he communicated with students, staff, and parents. He would discipline a student and they would thank him afterwards.

He was dedicated and very thorough. I once sent him to a class that had been acting up and told him to "read them the riot act." He returned in 30 minutes and was apologetic because he had looked everywhere in our admin office and could not locate a copy of the Riot Act. Ah, Marines, you gotta love 'em.

He was an excellent instructor of peer leadership and conflict resolution. Always respectful to the student, never raising his voice or demeaning in any way, he assured students that once the discipline was administered they would receive a fresh start. Parents seldom questioned his decisions and staff appreciated his quick response to their requests.

After he was there for one year, we received national recognition for our safety and security program. He is now an outstanding school principal, and there is one other thing he did well: he swept my daughter off her feet and became my son-in law. OOH-RAH! SEMPER FI!

I have found that, in a traditional classroom setting, Navy Junior Reserve Officer Training Corps instructors rarely need to call for help from an administrator. What's more, in my travels with Navy education programs I also discovered our instructors were frequently nominated for Teacher of the Year and were well respected by staff. I am sure results would be similar with our brother services. This is a far cry from wanting them off campus or condemning them for militarizing our children.

Consequences

I have found as a drill instructor and school teacher/administrator that there is value in discussing the importance of consequences for one's actions repeatedly with those in your charge. That's especially true because of the internet, where statements are made, then read by all before the originator has engaged his or her brain. Such actions can have lifelong negative effects. Besides teaching your field of expertise, you also have a responsibility to help your students mature so they can take advantage of opportunities for success. I urge you to engage in discussions on appropriate use of the internet as well as the impact of inappropriate information.

While most people will make a mistake or two, we should focus on prevention, and sharing our stories as veterans can be effective in explaining to students how unintended consequences can change and even ruin lives. You should try to pull from your time in service some effective examples to convey this lesson.

One incident from my deployment to the Caribbean on board the carrier Eisenhower demonstrated how acting without thought may result in unthinkable consequences. And it's an example that is easily understood by students.

We had a sailor who for one reason or another wanted out of the Navy. We will call him Seaman Schmuck. The Navy is an all-volunteer service, so we wondered why he joined in the first place. Hence the name.

Determined to obtain a discharge, Seaman Schmuck decided he would stage a suicide attempt by jumping overboard, indicating he was crazy and thus eligible for discharge. However, when he jumped from the flight deck, 80 feet above the water, he was wearing a life vest and made sure there were plenty of witnesses. Amazingly, he survived the fall and the ship sounded the "man overboard" alarm. We launched a helicopter with Navy rescue swimmers. As they were lowered into the water to hook Seaman Schmuck to a harness to be hoisted aboard the aircraft, sharks were sighted and it required us to hoist the swimmers at the same time, narrowly escaping a very bad scenario. Once on board, Seaman Schmuck was taken to medical. When he was found to be fit he was confined to the brig to await Captain's Mast Non-Judicial Punishment. A Navy vessel at sea is governed by maritime law and the commanding officer has the authority to sit as judge and administer punishment. The accused, along with his Division Officer, leading Chief, and I as Command Master Chief, report to the Captain. Plea, evidence, and recommendations are reviewed and the commanding officer may either dismiss or award different levels of punishment based on the Uniform Code of Military Justice, and may ultimately recommend a court martial.

Our Captain was prepared to grant the sailor his desired wish—a discharge from the service—under conditions other than honorable. However, he was also prepared to make a point to Seaman Schmuck and the rest of the crew of what the actual consequences may entail.

Seaman Schmuck stood at attention in front of the Captain and pleaded guilty to attempting suicide, endangering the crew and several other violations. The witnesses and I all agreed it would best for the Navy if Seaman Schmuck was discharged from active duty and sentenced to up to six months in the brig, along with a reduction in rank and a 50 percent reduction in pay for two months. The Captain agreed but wished to add one more detail. We began to discuss what Seaman Schmuck and the rest of us had not considered. A nuclear aircraft carrier cost approximately $1 million a day to operate, and it took an hour to save Seaman Schmuck. The cost was thus $41,666. The fuel for the helicopter was another $1000. There were six ships in our battle group that had to remain idle for one hour, costing another $60,000. Manslaughter charges would have been warranted had anything happened to our swimmers. So, American taxpayers were out a little over $102,000. On Seaman Schmuck's pay, if he were required to settle his debt before discharge, he would be in the brig for many years. You could hear his knees knock as he was considering his soon to be determined fate.

His final sentence was a reduction in rank, six months in

the brig, half pay for two months, and a discharge other than honorable from the Naval service.

Think before you act. Our Captain made his point. I have shared this story with every class since 1993 and it always receives rave reviews from students and is appreciated by parents.

Taking care of yourself

Physical fitness provides an edge when working with students. A teacher in excellent health seldom calls in sick or is off his or her game after a weekend. *They* are responsible for the class -- not a substitute who doesn't set the same standards. Students appreciate an instructor with high energy. Setting an example through proper nutrition and exercise is important for a young generation that is becoming increasingly sedentary.

Healthy teachers arriving at school on time and prepared for class is a virtue. And cafeteria duty qualifies as uncommon valor (I put that in for our Marine readers).

What time does the 0745 meeting start?

Punctuality is part of military life. The 0800 meeting starts at 0800, 0900 meeting at 0900, 1015 meeting at 1015, etc. It is the reason for the 24-hour clock versus p.m./a.m. – to eliminate confusion. In the military, which is engaged in the business of life or death, timing is critical. Developing the habit of being on time also is important to students, especially in an age where jobs are hard to come by.

At one school where I was principal, the parents became upset about our strict stance on tardiness. My predecessor had allowed it to become out of control and a laissez faire attitude prevailed when I arrived. Students were being dropped off late by parents because there was traffic, or they overslept. This was high school!

When I became principal, we would suspend students after three lates, as per the code of conduct, and parents were required to return with them for a conference. We would discuss with them the policy of one of our local banks for employees who are late the third time: dismissal. At a local university, the third late for class was forfeiture of tuition and the student had to repeat the class.

This approach had the desired effect. At the last school where I served as president, I would frequently use the PA system to ask my 1100 students, "What time do you show up for an 0800 meeting with the president?" and I would hear a resounding "0745, sir!"

Student discipline

In 20-plus years in public schools, I have observed many unsatisfactory approaches to addressing bad behavior. These incidents normally escalate into situations resulting in embarrassment to all concerned. Students are still adolescents, which means they can be a handful.

The movie *Lean on Me* is about Principal Joe Clark. He took the reins of a very undisciplined and out of control high school and whipped it into shape using some non-traditional methods of no-nonsense, strict discipline. He was successful, although controversial. Roaming the halls with a bullhorn, he was exciting to watch in action.

I am no Joe Clark. My methods differ greatly from his, which is not to say his were wrong, only that what works for one individual may not work as well for another. Joe Clark is not Chuck Baldwin either, and I believe my approach to discipline is equally effective. I like to call it the "parents' eye" technique.

This may sound familiar to you. When you were growing

up there may have been an incident of misbehavior where you were caught red-handed. When it came time to face the music it was never a pleasant experience. The sinking feeling in the stomach, the sweats, your mind racing, sure that your life is about to change drastically as Mom or Dad walked into the room. However, instead of the tongue lashing or discipline expected, they acted calmly and expressed their disappointment. Then came *the look*—the expression of disappointment. At that point, you went to your room. Nothing else needed to be said. Grounding, loss of phone privileges, early curfew—all seemed tame in comparison.

This scenario happens if there is respect, love, and admiration among all parties. The development of that emotional tie is up to you.

All veterans have had to become proficient in administering discipline. I never considered myself, nor should you, a rookie when I entered my first classroom. Depending upon your length of service, I would say you have at minimum a master's degree and quite possibly a doctorate in keeping order. This makes you a candidate to become an excellent teacher. Think about it: You have a class of 30 15-year-olds, all quiet and alert, who respect you. At that point, how hard can it be to teach? It is an awesome profession.

For a young teacher without experience other than a college class in classroom management and student teaching, defusing a conflict may be difficult. Going toe-to-toe with a student in front of friends usually translates to a situation described by an old Navy adage: "Constant bearing and decreasing range is a meeting situation." In other words, a collision is going to occur.

DPL number 5: Praise in Public and Reprimand in Private – is critical when interacting with students. Losing face in front of one's friends is horrifying for a young person. So, don't place them in that position. Take a young person off to the side, stand alongside him instead of toe-to-toe, and use a soft voice. That will usually produce positive results. It is what veterans have been taught to do with subordinates on active duty. And never be demeaning or disrespectful in your language. Adults do not like to be hurt with words, but they get over it; students take it much harder.

Another example on student interaction as it relates to discipline: Late spring is my favorite time of the school year: class rings, yearbook signings, preparing for finals, graduation, and the biggie—prom. I watch TV news in horror or read the insane columns in *Education Week* when the media discuss the issues surrounding this great event. Typical headlines are "What Will We Do about the Prom Dress Code?" or "Who is Authorized to Wear What," etc.

Let me break the news to everyone: no student wakes up the morning of prom and says, "Let me see how provocative or trashy I can look for the prom." They all want to look nice and do try very hard for this important occasion. I purposely greet each guest as they arrive and comment on how nice they look and tell them to have a great evening.

Now, do some of them push the envelope? Yes. There is always something too tight, too revealing, too garish, whatever. Inform the staff that, since you have seen all the students, they are fine to be at the dance. If they have an issue with the way a student is dressed, they are welcome to make note and meet with the student on Monday. At that time, let the student know that he or she was over the line and should have dressed a little more conservatively. Then suggest to the parents that they should speak with their child. Done. The prom is not the place to tell a young person he or she looks like garbage. I have attended 15 proms and have yet to observe anyone who was so far out of line they needed to be sent home.

I actually had a staff member tell a young lady she looked like a hooker and she should leave the dance immediately. The young lady had pushed the limit, but she was in no way obscene. At my direction, she was allowed to stay at the dance. What was obscene was ruining this young lady's special evening. Now,

I am sure there are many administrators and board members who will disagree with the way this was handled, but being a retired Command Master Chief I considered it a good job. BRAVO ZULU to me.

First steps toward your new career

As a veteran contemplating education as a possible second career, here are a few ideas to help you prepare:

1. If you are an E-6 or above and retiring, contact a JROTC program coordinator one year prior to retirement and initiate the teacher certification process.
2. See the Education Specialist at your command and have your military service evaluated for college credit. ACE Turner Guide evaluation.
3. Check out DANTES Troops to Teachers Program.
4. Take the College Level Examination Program (CLEP) exam.
5. If you are considering teaching in a field other than JROTC, check with the Department of Education in the state in which you are retiring for certification requirements one year prior to separation.
6. Certify for Master Training Specialist.
7. Brush up on your lectern skills.
8. Stay current with education technology tools.
9. Check out *Education Week* online for the latest news in education.
10. Contact your closest JROTC or check your local schools for veterans currently employed in teaching and solicit feedback on their experiences.
11. Enroll in college education related courses (School Law is especially helpful).
12. Enroll in courses related to the field you wish to teach.
13. Speak with a current teacher other than a JROTC instructor.

14. Consider substitute teaching if the opportunity presents itself.
15. Remember, get those shoes.

You have four years-plus in real world experience compared to what college grads are receiving in a class or while student teaching. Employ your skills wisely. Being well groomed and professional when you report for work should be second nature. Your principal will appreciate it, as will parents, students, and peers. As an educator, look the part. It's a wonderful profession, one for which you're well suited.

In the armed forces, work ethic training began after the oath. We are all one family with one mission. Unity, brotherhood, sisterhood are the guiding principles. Honor, Courage, Commitment, Integrity, and Valor are more than words. They are a way of life. As a veteran, when you carry those ideals into the civilian world you will find success and the local community welcoming, proud to have you serve once again.

If you are recently separated from the service and have been hired for that first teaching position, you are probably well versed in the basics. However, here are a few steps you may want to consider as you embark on your career as an educator:

1. If you have an assigned mentor, sit down with him or her and discuss approaches to classroom management.
2. Identify teachers in your school who are known for good classroom management and ask them to observe your class.
3. Have a discussion with your administrator on management techniques.
4. Get to know your students, identify potential class leaders and seat them strategically in your room.
5. Do not let issues get out of control. Do not hesitate to ask for help.

Special needs students and the Individuals with Disability Act and Rehabilitation Act of 1973

This act governs your responsibility to provide another service and understand a new acronym, FAPE—Free and Appropriate Public Education to persons with disabilities. In other words, a guaranteed right that you must ensure happens in your classroom.

Once a student has been diagnosed with a learning disability or physical handicap, he or she will be authorized to have an Individualized Education Plan (IEP). The plan is prepared by a team that includes the parents, the student, the school psychologist, nurse, administrator and teachers. It may require the student to be given special seating in the class, prompts to get him or her on task, extra time for testing, and permission to seek medical attention. I have had students with hearing loss and had someone in the class sign for them. At one school, there were two blind students and one in a wheelchair—all required special consideration.

After the IEP is decided upon, you must strictly adhere to it. It is reviewed periodically and parents may ask for a meeting to discuss progress at any time. The important thing is that the student must receive an education.

If you are new to public education you may be surprised at the number of students in this category. They are not a burden; they are deserving young men and women who have been dealt a different hand. You will have teachers in your school certified in special education. Seek them out if you have issues. If you have a school psychologist, get to know him or her and follow their advice.

A similar case is for someone on what they call a 504 plan. This covers cases where the disabling condition is not severe. It may be asthma or ADD (attention deficit disorder), for example. The student will have a modified plan agreed upon at a meeting with the same individuals as in the IEP, with the possible exception of the psychologist. Again, you must follow these guidelines.

Including these students and not making them feel like outsiders is your responsibility. Welcome them to your class as you would any student. You may be surprised at what you learn from them and how it will make you a better teacher.

A common mistake made by many educators is informing a struggling or difficult student's parents that they may wish to consider having the student tested for special education services. The minute you make the recommendation, the school is required to conduct testing—at considerable cost—and you will not be real popular with the administration. You are not a psychologist. The proper procedure is to let the administration know and he or she will decide, along with the psychologist, if testing is required before making a recommendation to parents.

As Commandant of the Delaware Military Academy, I was blessed with many of these wonderful kids. One in particular stands out. He was among the first cadets we accepted at our new school. Michael had cerebral palsy. He was highly intelligent but physically challenged. The Academy JROTC program had a requirement of a bi-annual physical fitness test of push-ups, sit-ups and a one-and-a-half-mile run. All students at the Academy are in the JROTC program. Although Michael could not participate in those exercises, the Military Science instructors wanted to make sure he had a challenging exam. They designed exercises that were tough for him and pushed him to his physical limits. As he took the test, the other cadets cheered him on. They absorbed great life lessons in kindness and fellowship in their interactions with Michael. Our staff was proud and it made us work even harder with those cadets who had unique circumstances.

When Mike turned 16 he became eligible for driver's ed. The nearest facility that could test him was in another state. The financial cost of sending him there and paying for the test was major but worth every penny, and he became just like all the other guys in his class.

Mike had one other fantastic skill: he was an awesome DJ, and we hired him for our school dances. He became quite a celebrity. My proudest moment as a Commandant was presenting him with his diploma after four great years.

CHAPTER 6

· · · · · · ●●● ● ●●● · · · · · ·

Know Your Students DPL 6, 8 and 9

Respect yourself and others will respect you.

Confucius

In the military, enlisted personnel salute officers as a sign of respect for their rank. It is one of my favorite regulations. There is nothing better than to begin your day with a cheerful and respectful greeting. At military schools, bases, and ships, salutes are a constant re-enforcement of "I respect you and respect is returned." As Command Master Chief, I periodically would have to address a young officer who failed to return a salute, and after I explained the importance of recognizing those who are respecting you, they seldom repeated the offense.

The salute is a form of greeting, and for veterans it becomes a part of everyday life. You will find this will be a huge asset in a school setting. Students enjoy being recognized. Part of my morning principal routine once I completed bus duty was to stop by each homeroom and wish the students a great day. When I worked as a teacher I made it a point to speak with as many students as I could—even those not in my classes. This puts you in a positive light, and once you are viewed that way by the student body, you will be surprised at how much you can accomplish and how easy it is to correct behavior.

As a veteran, you should review your branch of service Uniform Regulations regarding wearing the uniform. If you are teaching JROTC you will be in uniform, if teaching another discipline, you will be in civvies. Retirees on occasion are authorized to wear the uniform. I typically would wear mine on the Navy or Marine Corps Birthday, Veterans Day, and Memorial Day. Bring your uniform to class and spend time going over the rank, insignias, patches, ribbons, and medals. This is a great ice breaker at the beginning of the year and it starts the kids on a path of becoming familiar with the new teacher. Remember, they are students, so stay away from the bloody war stories. Keep it civil—and civilized.

That is not to say you should never draw upon your experiences to enhance your lesson plan or inject appropriate humor in your interactions. World travels are always interesting and military lifestyle is a great topic. Many of your students have veterans in their families and may have some idea of that lifestyle. For the most part, however, you represent the military to them and you will play an important role in forming their opinion of military service. You have an opportunity to provide truth through fact and experience. If not for the veteran, the student would have to rely on Hollywood, the internet and media, which do not always portray our servicemen and women in the best light.

DPL 9 Have your students know you. If someone attempts to tell you that your job is to "teach them and not be their friend," my recommendation is to smile, wish that person a good day, and never accept advice from them again. I was friends with the most junior sailor on a nuclear aircraft carrier and with the toughest kid in school.

If you take away one thing from this book, it should be **DPL6: All students are great children and your job as**

a professional educator is to mentor them and provide instruction and guidance in the educational journey, placing them on a steady course to success and good citizenship. Do not pass judgment. Embrace them.

I enjoy knowing my students not only inside but outside the classroom. Twice I took 10 students to Taiwan for two weeks on a school exchange program. Three times a year I would take 15 students on a weekend camping and climbing trip and always volunteered to assist as chaperone on teacher-sponsored field trips (teachers appreciated having the principal along). The more time I spent with students the better we interacted. Students who went mountain climbing with me always reacted and responded to me in a positive manner. The level of equal respect was high.

DPL 8: Know your students. This piece of advice may seem old school, but it works. As a teacher or administrator, it should be on your to do list to learn their names, quickly, and to use them. Stay away from nicknames because you can never be sure how they feel about them. Have a seating chart for your class with the first name of the student in large, bold letters (larger as you get older). Each time you interact with them, place a tick mark next to the name. It will assist you in learning their names and help identify communication patterns. For example, you may discover that you call on one part of the room more frequently than another.

Now, I'm not recommending that you take your class to Taiwan for two weeks. The point is, you should try to get to know them both in and outside of class. It may be something as simple as a pizza party after school in the cafeteria or attending a sports practice.

Your level of commitment to them is part of the respect equation.

A sailor came to my office one day while we were in port and invited me to his son's baptism that Sunday. I was what is known in the Navy as a geographical bachelor. My family lived in Delaware and I lived on the ship in Virginia during the week, going home on weekends. To a young sailor, the Command Master Chief represents the top of the line in the enlisted community. I certainly wanted to be at home and see my wife and children on the weekend but after weighing how important it would be for this young sailor to have me at the baptism, it was an easy decision: I was going to church. Of course, the word spread and there were many more invitations in the future for the rest of my tour, but I always felt it an honor and a responsibility. My wife got over it and we are still together after 43 years.

That same level of commitment is important to students. Much like sailors, they will extend invitations to you, especially at graduation time. As a principal, you will be invited to many graduation parties. My rule to the staff was, if you accept one invitation to a graduation party, you must accept all. There is nothing worse than to attend student A's graduation party while ignoring students B, C, and D. Graduates go from party to party, and trust me, they know where you have been. Once the "all or nothing" rule was established, most teachers opted for nothing.

Not me. My secretary would RSVP to all, then set up a MapQuest itinerary. I would spend the day and evening stopping at each location for five to ten minutes. Parents, grandparents, and relatives were appreciative, and as a bonus I had the opportunity to wish my grads well face-to-face.

To sum up, the formula that has worked well for me as a principal and teacher is:

Structure and discipline + sound academic principles + love and respect = outstanding citizens.

CHAPTER 7

· · · · · · · ●●● ● ●● · · · · · · · ·

Moral Courage

*The truth of the matter is that you always know
the right thing to do. The hard part is doing it.*

Gen. Norman Schwarzkopf

One weakness I find in the public school system is the lack of
moral courage. Normally only seasoned educators are willing
to stand up to authority and express their views. Political
correctness seems to be a way of life with inexperienced
educators, and that is certainly understandable if they do not
have the deckplate experience of a veteran. If you have served
in the military, however, you are more likely to have developed
the courage and knowledge to understand that it is always
better to do the right thing.

Telling the emperor he is naked does indeed require
courage. But once you have a true understanding of leadership,
you discover how valuable it is to speak the truth, regardless of
supposed consequences. The book *Team of Rivals,* by Doris
Kearns Goodwin, describes how President Lincoln appointed
a Cabinet made up of individuals unafraid to speak their minds.
This was an outstanding demonstration of moral courage. If you

think standing up to your boss is tough, just imagine standing up to Abraham Lincoln.

Young teachers are not the only ones who need training in this area. As I said earlier, military veterans have been exposed to it, but that does not necessarily make them Captains Courageous. An incident from my service on board the Dwight D. Eisenhower illustrates that point.

Every day in port we held a meeting at 5 p.m. known as HODS (Heads of Departments). That included 18 senior officers, the Commanding Officer, the Executive Officer, and I, as Command Master Chief. One evening, our Captain presented us with a proposal for a Dependents Cruise, in which the ship goes to sea for a day and provides entertainment, an air show, and a cookout for the families and friends of the crew. Typically, 8,000 plus attend this event. To organize and prepare an aircraft carrier for such an event requires days of labor. We had recently returned from a six-month deployment and several local exercises, so we were tired of spending our days at sea.

The Captain wanted everyone's input, so in round-table style each department head voiced his opinion, either in favor or opposed. Not surprisingly, opposed was unanimous. Finally, the Captain looked at me and asked for my thoughts. I told him I was all for it and the crew would love a day showing off our great ship. He agreed and scheduled the cruise. As we left the meeting it was evident I had just lost 18 friends.

One month later we left port with thousands of our loved ones. We enjoyed live bands, movies and activities for the kids, a magnificent air show, tours of the ship, awesome food, and a wonderful day at sea. As I departed the ship that evening I was approached, one by one, by all 18 Department Heads, who thanked me for making the right call. Sometimes, moral courage means being in the minority.

Command

When in charge of an organization you must be just that, in charge. I discovered quickly after becoming a public school principal that command in the military and command in the school system are two different animals. Superintendents, assistant superintendents, school boards, and even well connected parents were all playing a role in my daily life as head of school—and not a very positive one.

Imagine the commander of a nuclear aircraft carrier, tank unit, aircraft, or Marine landing force checking with five or six groups for permission before executing commands. It's unfortunate, but many of our schools are exactly in that situation and we continue to lose some top commanders (principals) as a result. This is just one more indicator of the need for strong military leaders in our education system to help us get back on course.

When I was interviewed for the position of principal, I was asked if I would commit to five years. Consistency being a good thing, I assured them that would not be a problem. My only request was to have input into the selection of the two assistant principals. The following week the mailman delivered a two-year contract that contained the names of my two new assistants. When I asked the board about the two years instead of five, I was told it was standard policy and they wished to monitor my performance. I was also told the two assistants had already been selected by the district office, a policy that had been followed previously. I also was asked to prepare a 50-page paper on how to improve state-mandated test scores. I was not authorized to address curriculum since that is a responsibility of the district assistant superintendent in charge of curriculum. They also informed me of next year's budget and teaching staff. I was knowledgeable about the state calculations for these figures, and I found them to be way off in terms of both money and staff. When I responded to that effect, district administrators advised me that they had their own formula.

So, students I had never met were performing poorly on curricula I did not select and the people who were going to help me were unknown to me, on both a personal and professional level. What's more, I would receive operating funds and staffing well below what the state's calculations indicated they should be. While I was taking this in, I received an emergency call from the district office; a board member's child had not been picked up by the bus and she demanded an explanation. Welcome to public school administration. I sent my two-year contract back with a note saying I was no longer committed to five years, but to two.

Working at the school was a joy and I loved the kids, but never in two years felt in charge. I was never provided information about contracts regarding the building structure or transportation, and knew I would not be there long enough to discharge anyone for poor teaching since they were all tenured. Discipline decisions could be appealed to the district and financial accountability and staffing were confusing.

Public Charter School

Goodbye, traditional public school, hello, public charter school. What a difference in responsibility and command. Responsibility is the key word. If you do poorly, you close, if you run out of money, you close, if students do not enroll, you close, if you do not achieve your charter objectives, you close.

The head of the school is aware of how much is spent on everything: transportation, athletic coaches, utilities, staff—everything. When I would leave my traditional public school at night I would go out to my car and head home. At a charter public school, before leaving you make sure there are no faucets leaking and the lights are off and doors locked, because you must pay the bills.

And there are no cuts in staffing. Teachers ask what if there is a reduction in force? No problem, we close. Operating at the minimum makes it very easy. We have enough staff to teach the students we have, no more. Board members of the charter are well informed and understand their role as a corporate board. They must acquire resources for the corporation (the school) to be successful. Micro management of the school leader is not in their wheelhouse. Charter schools that have boards acting like public school boards do not obtain adequate resources, thus ensuring the failure of the school. The school leader must be allowed to command and be the primary decision maker. He or she must work with the board to identify needs, keep the board informed, include the board in major capital decisions, and ensure the school is strictly adhering to the charter. And duties do not include picking up a board member's child who was late for the bus.

A later chapter will provide a thorough review of the regulations and policies governing policies specific to charter schools.

Communicating bad news

One of the most difficult tasks for anyone in a leadership position is to communicate unpleasant news. Many people today use email or text message or other social media to communicate bad news. Let me assure you these are not appropriate methods when an individual student is involved. In fact, I don't even like to use the telephone. Bad news is best delivered in person. If you are shy about doing that, you probably should find a position that doesn't require you to deal with the public or have any subordinates. Bad news will happen and effectively communicating it is an essential skill for a leader.

Electronic mail and the telephone are good for one-way, initial communication to set up face-to-face appointments, but not for discussions of a serious nature. Every day at schools around the country there are major issues resulting from improper, imprecise electronic communications, causing unnecessary grief to all concerned.

In public schools nowadays, this is the scenario that typically unfolds: When an incident occurs, a student immediately calls home on his cell and briefs the parent before an investigation can be conducted. The student, of course, provides only his version of events. This is usually followed by a call to the principal from an angry parent that normally begins with "How dare you?" If I were the student I would probably do the same thing. It's a great way to limit damage and obtain an ally.

Over the years, I have learned a few tricks of the trade, so let me suggest a path to a constructive solution.

Whenever a serious event occurs and the guilty party has been identified, before consequences are administered, have the student report to the administrative conference room. Contact the parents and ask them to come to the school. Once parents arrive, greet them and escort them to the conference room. Ask the student to describe the incident. If there are witnesses to the incident, have their statements ready, or evidence necessary to contradict. When students are caught red-handed they normally provide a fairly accurate account of what transpired.

By this time, the parents are somewhat subdued and want to know what happens next. Show them the Code of Conduct, opened to the page of possible consequences for the violation. At this point it becomes relatively easy to come to an agreement on disciplinary action. Parents are happy they were included, the student feels remorse, you can create a positive resolution and chalk it up to a learning experience for all concerned.

While social media is not appropriate when individual students are involved, it is effective when a major event occurs. In that case—after you have gathered all the facts—employ every available communication tool to make sure parents know all is under control, or, if there is a danger, what course of action they should take. Do not skew the facts or leave out anything. It is your duty as the custodian of their children to provide them with the absolute truth.

Here again, moral courage must be a guiding principle. That means being willing to admit when you are wrong. Administrators, teachers, and parents are not perfect by any means. Seldom is there a need to raise your voice to a student, but if you have done so, apologize to that student and his parents. If you have falsely accused a student, or been demeaning in any way, apologize. The apology alone is a good lesson for a young person. When you are wrong, step up and do not attempt to camouflage. The more open and honest you are the better you will be able to lead.

CHAPTER 8

· · · · · ●●●● ● ●●●●● · · · · ·

Project Based Learning

If we teach today's students as we taught students of yesterday, we will rob them of tomorrow.

John Dewey, American Philosopher and Educational Reformer

In 2011, I took a position with an organization seeking to bring successful school models to the state of Delaware for replication. Innovation is not the strong suit of the public school system in general, but this is especially so in Delaware. Many of our schools have not adopted new curricula or pedagogy in decades. Even Montessori, an outstanding program that has proven itself for more than 100 years, is not available to all our citizens. We need to do better.

In my new position, I was able to travel around the United States and visit effective school programs in order to bring those models to Delaware. I visited Early College High School in Ohio and NewTech Network in Texas. I traveled to California, Indiana and New York (Project Based Learning) and to The Met Big Picture School in Rhode Island. All of them were outstanding.

After visiting these schools, I was shocked that we in

Delaware had nothing like them, even though these school models had been in use and successful for many years.

I apparently wasn't very good at my job because I had trouble convincing anyone to try these programs. More bothersome was the fact that our organization, a private education think tank, was checking out these programs and not my District Board of Education and the State Department of Education. Thank goodness for Delaware State University and its outstanding leadership. They knew the value of the Early College High School model. DSU stepped up to the plate and established an Early College Charter School on its campus. When you have an opportunity, I suggest you go online and learn how the program is helping first generation college students. And, if they are asking for donations, I hope you are able to contribute.

What was most disappointing was the failure to open and grow The Met school in our state. Founded in Providence, R. I., the Met schools are now located all over the U.S. and several foreign countries. What they accomplish is remarkable. They enroll students who are struggling and have failed in the traditional public school setting and place them in PBL programs and internships.

Their graduation rate is 100 percent. Programs like the Met should be nurtured and replicated. You can review the program online, and if you are an educator you may want to schedule a visit to the Providence campus.

One bright light on the horizon is the First State Military Academy(FSMA) in Clayton, Del. In July of 2012 I was enjoying myself on the beach in sunny Italy when I received a call from U.S. Senator Tom Carper of Delaware inquiring if I would be interested in speaking with Scott Kidner, from Dover, Del., about starting a military academy like DMA. I told the senator yes and as soon as I returned to the U.S. I contacted Mr. Kidner. The result is a Marine Corps Military Academy Charter High School that has partnered with the New Tech Network and offers a curriculum delivering Project Based Learning. At

FSMA, students work on year-long projects in groups using technology. Each problem is required to have history, English, math and science components.

PBL assignments in traditional New Tech schools are real world. I visited one of their best schools, in Austin, Texas, where the students were all working on the levee problem in New Orleans following Hurricane Katrina. They were engaged and excited about helping the community. Similarly, at FSMA, they are in the process of requesting real-world problems from the Marine Corps and having the cadets come up with solutions. R&D at no cost! Who knows? Maybe the cadets will find a solution to reduce the weight of a Marine's pack. I am convinced real world PBL projects are the future for education.

The best schools in America require advanced research projects in the junior or senior years. Ivy League schools and other leading universities have been telling school systems for some time that students need to be problem solvers and know how to integrate disciplines. Scoring high on the SAT to get in and then dropping out in December is not cutting it. If there is a school in your area that has students engaged in PBL, investigate. If not, go online and set up a time to explore the New Tech Network and possibly arrange a visit. If, upon review, you feel PBL may be a pedagogy worth trying, enroll in training opportunities. The value of inquiry and investigative components of PBL are exciting and will leave you eager to try it with your students.

CHAPTER 9

· · · · · ● ● ● ● ● ● ● ● ● · · · · · ·

The Community Solution

Alone we are smart, together we are brilliant.

Steven Anderson, Educator

Schools—especially charter schools—must reach beyond their walls to achieve success. And parents, above all, are your most important allies.

Educators hear repeatedly that for a student to be successful, you must have engaged parents. In fact, we educators are the ones saying it most often. Unfortunately, a typical school in the United States does little to engage parents.

Here's how a day unfolds at a school of 1200 students: Students go to a bus stop within steps of their home and are delivered to school, where they participate in the breakfast program. Then it's off to class. At noon, they go to the cafeteria and purchase lunch or have it provided, depending on family economics. Then it's back to class. At the end of the day, buses take some students home while others stay to participate in our free after school program. That includes free snacks at 4 p.m.

At 4:30, buses take those students home. That evening, the parent can go online to see if little Johnny did his work.

This typical day has created a situation in which parents really have no need to engage—unless they happen to believe it's necessary.

As educators, we must be innovators. Parent engagement is critical, so how do we navigate these waters without washing up on the shoals of disengagement? Answer: make them feel welcome at your school.

Here are several ideas to help create parent engagement:

1. Set up parent conferences so they are convenient for the parent. Scheduling on a weekday before 5 p.m. is a guarantee they probably will not be able to attend.
2. Publish weekly electronic bulletins to all parents with reminders of school activities.
3. Hold a Grandparents Day.
4. Schedule a lunch at the school once or twice a month for five or six parents and eat in the cafeteria. You will horrify their children, but it's an effective way of engaging the parents in their children's school day.
5. In some schools, notices of interim reports are still sent by snail mail. Send them electronically. It's much faster, timelier, and eliminates the potential of the report being "lost in the mail."
6. The PTA stands for Parent *Teacher* Association. It's been my experience that many of them have evolved into *Parent* organizations. Teachers and administrators who complain about parent engagement should examine closely how active they have been in this activity.
7. Institute a program to recognize a parent or volunteer of the month.
8. Student recognition must be widely publicized. A note in the weekly bulletin congratulating honor roll students is not enough.

9. When a ceremony is conducted to recognize student accomplishments, be sure it is well organized and is presented with polish.
10. Standing outside and performing arrival and departure duty has real value. Parents appreciate seeing you, and on many occasions I have had parents stop for a brief conversation.
11. Invite parents to view student project presentations.

If you are working in a traditional public school you need to learn that in today's environment your parent must also go by another name: *client*. Private, parochial, and public charters are aware of the importance of client/school relations. Their experience affords them an edge in the intense competition for enrollment.

Now that we have achieved parental engagement, let's turn our attention to the business community. This is a relatively easy task. You will probably find the local Chamber of Commerce ready and willing to form a partnership. Projects, internships, field trips, guest speaking engagements, school visits and much more are yours for the asking. But you *must* ask. Once you do, how can they object? After all, you are training their future employees, and it's in their best interest to help you succeed.

Years ago, aboard the aircraft carrier, I discovered a unique way to reach out to the community: placemats. I would use my resume as a placemat when hosting VIP meals.

When I became a school administrator I adopted the idea of using placemats to spread the word about the school. We made up placemats featuring students' work, including math, art, and essays. Several local restaurants agreed to use them (names removed, of course, for all you litigators). It went over well; members of the community enjoyed looking at student work and commenting on the level of excellence. This was during a time when negative editorials on public school students' performance were all too common. It became a source of pride for teachers and students to have their work displayed. This is just one example of how schools can market themselves and the good work they accomplish.

And as noted earlier, USEED is a great fundraising tool. But it also helps engage the entire community. I had an opportunity to use it for the First State Military Academy, and we recruited 171 participants, including traditional public schools, local police, the business community, parents, staff members, board members, military units (all branches), veterans organizations, and—get this—government officials. We accepted all donations, no matter how small, and those who could not afford to give contacted a friend who did. The result—the one-of-a-kind obstacle course—will be a source of pride for the entire community.

I am convinced the future of education is going to have to go in this direction, where everyone has a stake in the game and may actively participate in many ways. It would be wonderful if leadership could come up with a solution to funding, but if we are honest with ourselves we know it is not going to happen in the near future. Meanwhile, we cannot sit and wait while students go without. Programs like USEED, with no up-front money required, offer opportunities to improve our schools and our educational system while engaging the community – now.

CHAPTER 10

• • • • • • •●● ● ●● • • • • • • • •

Navy Junior Reserve Officer Training Corps

I can imagine no more rewarding a career. And any man who may be asked in this century what he did to make his life worthwhile, I think can respond with a great deal of pride and satisfaction: "I served in the United States Navy."

John F. Kennedy,
President of the United States

In my professional life, I have been blessed with a great deal of success. Several notable achievements stand out: promotion to Chief Petty Officer and Master Chief Petty Officer; Command Master Chief of CVN 69 USS Dwight D. Eisenhower; a final four candidate for Master Chief Petty Officer of the Navy, and Master's Degree in School Leadership and Instruction. However, my certification as a Navy JROTC instructor was the best day of my professional life. After a fantastic military career, it was difficult for me to determine "what now"? There couldn't be anything as exciting or rewarding as serving my country, travelling around the world, living the Navy adventure. Truck driving, welding, store manager, movie star are all respectable vocations, but not something I wanted to do for a second career. Well, maybe movie star.

I always had a knack for connecting with young people, so I decided that education may be the way to go. I applied and was hired to open a Navy JROTC program in Seaford, Del., in June of 1993, to begin work in July, immediately upon completion of NIOT (New Instructor Orientation Training).

The training was outstanding and although I had never been in a high school setting with students, I felt comfortable with the support systems the Navy had in place and confident I could perform the job. One variable made me somewhat wary, however. I discovered my partner and boss was going to be a Marine, Lt. Col. Glynn Hodges. I've always respected and admired Marines and often boast about never having come across a bad one. Working for one, though, might be a whole different proposition.

Not so. The colonel was organized, disciplined, hard-working and dedicated to making our program a success, as was I. We had each other's backs from day one and I carried on the time-honored tradition of making sure my boss always looked good in the performance of our unit. Trucks would arrive with loads of uniforms and books and he would roll up his sleeves and we would work side by side. We kept our area manager informed, turned our paperwork in on time, conducted thorough inventories, maintained a positive working relationship with Pensacola HQ, communicated with established programs, and, most important, made ourselves known to the local community—all items that were covered in detail at NIOT.

In dealing with the chain of command in a school setting, one problem you should be aware of is the possibility of some teachers and administrators attempting to subvert that chain. They may, for instance, ask you to perform a task or provide assistance and expect an answer before you check with your partner/superior. Thanks to our military training, it was policy that both the colonel and I must be made aware of any evolution involving the unit. When I moved on to my career in education, the teacher or administrator looking to deal with me rather than my tough boss was often taken aback by my refusal. Too bad. We were a team and divisiveness was not part of the plan.

Years later while I was working at another unit an incident occurred at a JROTC located several miles from my school that serves as a good example of not having each other's back. I received a call one morning from an E-9 wanting to share "how dumb his colonel was." He said they had a unit field trip organized that was scheduled to depart at 0800. After waiting for 15 minutes for transportation, they called the bus company and discovered the colonel who had agreed to set up transportation had failed to do so. He dropped the ball—as we all have at one time or another. The E-9 repeated, "How stupid can you be?"

I replied, "Obviously, not as stupid as you." Why hadn't there been any follow up? Didn't they speak to each other? Why didn't they have a check-off list? The whole unit suffered, cadets missed an important educational field trip, man hours were lost in organization, and the unit appeared disorganized in the eyes of school administration and JROTC peers. Perhaps most important, parents were upset -- all because Tweedledum and Tweedledee were not on the same page. Now you know why I referred to him not by name but as an E-9.

That was 25 years ago. My colonel is long since retired but we remain in touch. I learned a great deal about education from my partner. We played off each other's strengths and as a result had a wonderful time at work and, more important, we had a very successful unit.

As an NJROTC instructor I have been involved in four start-up units—three Navy and one Marine. All presented unique challenges as well as one major common issue: cadet recruitment. There are many variables that go into a successful recruitment program, including location, school support, competition, and program activities.

It's important to remember that no young person is going to join your program to simply sit and listen to the JROTC curriculum, get yelled at, and do push-ups. Program activities are vital to your success. Drill teams, color guards, orientation trips, fun stuff, leadership camps, community service projects— all are part of the experience. Many of these have financial obligations. One caution: Keep in mind the cost of activities. Some students may shy away from joining a unit if they think what they wish to do is unaffordable.

A quick way to failure in recruiting students is to not deliver on what you have offered in your marketing. If you advertise orientation flights, drill competitions, and leadership camps, make sure you follow through with those promises.

I am not a current NIOT Instructor and have been out of the active JROTC business for quite some time, so it's not prudent for me to provide detailed advice regarding rules and regulations since the programs are always changing. I am, however, still involved with the Marine Academy, which brings me endless joy. Allow me to share what you have to look forward to now that you are an educator in an outstanding program:

1. Cadets receiving scholarships, appointments, college acceptances, jobs, and enlisting in the military. In other words, young people becoming productive members of society.

2. Phone calls from parents expressing their thanks for what you do for their children.

3. Education professionals appreciating your skill set. I can't tell you how many times teachers have come to me and asked for help with a cadet who is acting up in their class. (I would love to take one of my cadets to the

Spanish teacher who has a child in my class and ask that teacher for assistance with disciplining the student).

4. Great support from your chain of command and the JROTC staffs.
5. Access to wonderful learning opportunities.
6. A lengthy Christmas card list.
7. Graduations, baptisms, weddings, christenings, confirmations, and lots of phone calls from former cadets.

Another item for you to focus on as an educator is your continuing education. Many public school districts offer tuition assistance. If not, if you are fortunate enough to have dollars remaining in your GI bill, use them toward another certification or specific teaching skill. You will impress your administrator as well as enhance your abilities. As a result of your military service you are well prepared for classroom management, but there are always new tricks to learn that make your job teaching cadets a more enjoyable experience for you and your students.

Having a plan B is important. Budgetary issues—both state and federal—reduced enrollment, and local politics are always factors to keep in mind. I don't want to scare anyone, but what happens if your program were to be dropped? Having the education and a certification to fall back on relieves anxiety. Be prepared for a change in job description also. When I enrolled in courses to become an administrator the plan was not to leave the classroom. Boy, did I underestimate the respect afforded former military and their discipline skills. The day after I received an administrator's certification they transferred me to an assistant principal position in a middle school of 1100 seventh and eighth graders. Thank God I was a Vietnam and Persian Gulf veteran!

If you are new to the program, don't be shy or afraid to speak up. It's okay even for big folks to call a TTO (training time out). Anxiety is not a fun feeling, but help is a phone call, email, tweet away. Your fellow JROTC Instructors are among your best resources.

My respect and admiration to all who are taking this journey.

CHAPTER 11

· · · · · ·••• ● •••• · · · ·

If you build it, they will indeed come: The Delaware Military Academy

School is a building which has four walls with tomorrow inside.

Lon Watters, Educator and Artist

On July 4, 2001, I attended a cookout at the home of Lt. Col. Jack Wintermantel, a friend of many years and close associate during my tenure as a JROTC instructor. We were both lamenting the state of education and the need for more JROTCs and military schools in general. My concern with military schools was that they were so expensive to attend and most of the students were not military. A tuition-free charter military school open to young women and men who desire to attend based upon military interest would be a great idea if:

1. You had the property.
2. You had a charter.
3. You had branch of service JROTC approval.
4. You had $15 million for construction.
5. You had branch of service agreement to sponsor uniforms for all cadets to wear daily.
6. You had 500 or more cadets.
7. You had a corporation and 501(c)(3) tax status.
8. You had community buy-in.
9. You had a curriculum aligned with state standards.

We discussed the above and concluded that, with the two of us working together, we might be able to accomplish our dream. Both of us were employed, I as a principal and he as Director of Logistics for the Delaware National Guard. This would require us to quit our jobs and go for a time without income. My military retirement and a small grant for charter start-ups would keep me in beans and allow me to begin the monumental task. The colonel would have to wait for a few months before our scheduled opening in 2003—if we were successful—to leave his position.

The property—and community buy-in

We hit a roadblock right away in searching for a location. As part of the charter process we were required to present our charter to the State Board of Education. They thought we had a wonderful idea but voted that morning for a one-year moratorium on new charter schools. This could have ended our quest because the Navy had agreed to grant us a Navy JROTC program for the year 2003 and if there was a moratorium we would have to reapply. The plan would only work if the charter, the NJROTC program, and building construction coincided.

On the way out the door, the Secretary of Education indicated that this would not preclude us from applying for a district charter, although only one district in the state would accept such requests. If we were granted a charter it would have to be located within that district's borders. Fortunately, there was a four-acre piece of property located near a park in that district that was ideal. It was zoned industrial and we had to go through the process of rezoning and public hearing with the neighborhood. During the hearing, several people spoke against our proposal, based on an increase in traffic and noise. The Department of Land Use ruled in our favor and lifted the zoning restriction.

The Charter

Writing a charter application is a daunting task. Aspects of your school operations, staffing, financing, curriculum, transportation, discipline, special education, meals, custodial procedures, and extracurricular activities must be addressed. We submitted our application to the school district, attended numerous hearings, both public and private, and presented the objectives of the charter. The board agreed to a five-year charter with an annual financial audit and review of our objectives.

Building construction

The hard work was about to begin. Constructing a school for 500-plus cadets and providing the necessary resources would cost $12 million. The builder, Paul Talley, listened to our proposal and was convinced that this was a solid idea that would be great for young men and women. He agreed to build the school for a reasonable and affordable rent with an offer to buy once we were established. All the risk was on him. He went to work on the building and we went to work recruiting 300 cadets for grades 9 and 10 our opening year, with plans to increase enrollment and include grades 11 and 12 in subsequent years.

The Navy

Receiving authorization for a Navy JROTC unit was essential if we were to have a Delaware Military Academy. Pensacola, Fla., is where the program is located and we went there in person to present the idea. Typically, an NJROTC unit has two instructors, one officer and one enlisted, and 100-120 cadets who are required to wear the uniform one day a week. To accept our proposal, they would have to agree to 500-plus cadets, seven instructors, and enough uniforms to wear every day of the week – all of which represented a big cost and an even bigger gamble. This had been attempted before in much larger locations with limited success. Maybe our passion showed through, because they agreed to grant our NJROTC, aligned with the proposal. *Go Navy!*

Today the Delaware Military Academy is the largest NJROTC full-time program in the U.S. Navy, with an enrollment of 584 cadets in grades 9-12. More impressive is that in the tiny state of Delaware we have more than 200 on the waiting list each year.

Recruiting

Depending on who you ask, between 10 and 20 percent of high school graduates may someday associate themselves in some way with the U.S. military. The local area was graduating 15,000 students each year. On the low end, that meant there were 1500 cadets in the market. There were also students looking for a school with fewer disruptions and one that would be safe. We worked out of the trunk of our cars as we attempted to reach the magic number of 300 by convincing students and parents we were the real thing and would indeed open on time and deliver on promised services. Four months before opening day we hit the magic number, and on opening day we actually had 320.

501(c)(3)

A 501(c)(3) is a document issued by the Internal Revenue Service granting an organization non-profit status and tax exemption. Normally it requires at least six months for approval. It is impossible to raise money without one because it is the first thing requested by possible donors. A call to your friendly U.S. Senator helps if your cause is just and your need urgent. We received ours in two weeks after one such call.

Curriculum

Experience as a school principal helped me to design the curriculum and class schedules. JROTC was a mandatory class each day. We received approval for our Department of Education to grant credit for companion courses aligned with the Navy standard curriculum, including such subjects as Drill and Ceremonies and Leadership.

MAP your day

I brought to DMA a program, MAP, developed while I was on active duty aboard the IKE. Becoming increasingly concerned with physical fitness of sailors (mine included) and a rise in conduct violations, I realized an improvement plan was necessary. Addressing those issues, I added an academic component to assist sailors with promotion chances. The sailors and their leadership responded well and the result was an increase in exercise classes, promotions, and improved behavior patterns. The commanding officer, Capt. William Cross, was an exceptional leader and he enhanced the program by placing an emphasis on unit pride. Being an IKE sailor had a special meaning. Our sailors were physically fit, morally correct, advanced before others and whether on board in a professional capacity or on shore on liberty, we set the example for excellence. I don't get to speak with Admiral Cross much anymore, but his lessons in developing subordinates have been the cornerstone for success for hundreds of my students. I hear often from former students that they still MAP out their day. *Bravo Zulu, Admiral!*

MAP is an acronym for Moral, Academic and Physical – a program of personal development. It requires participants to develop a habit of completing a daily task in each of these three areas, thus "mapping" their day.

Morally they should consider doing something nice for someone, perhaps by paying it forward. It may be something as simple as taking out the trash or as involved as a community service project.

Academically they may read a book or an article in a magazine, attend a lecture, view a documentary, go to the museum or the zoo, engage in a debate, etc.

Physically they may play catch, go for a run, or, when a commercial comes on, instead of eating a Twinkie, do 10 push-ups. Strong minds and bodies work well together.

It's a simple concept that can easily become habit. All the exercises are aimed at improving mind, body, and soul.

Unit pride is as important in a school as it is in the military. A school brimming with pride is typically well disciplined, organized, full of high academic achievers and the pride of the community. It's contagious, and parents, teachers, and administrators will follow suit.

Detractors of the initiative have told me that students acting better than others is arrogant. I disagree. Being proud of your success, behaving properly, and studying hard are all intrinsic values and not arrogant in any way. The students do not boast that they are better, but they are great kids.

CHAPTER 12

· · · · · •••• ● ••••• · · · ·

Resource Opportunities

When I drive by a park and see a broken swing set all I really see is an opportunity for an engineering and community service project for my students.

Chuck Baldwin

As an educator in a world of denied resources, it is difficult to engage and challenge our high-energy students. If your students are not high-energy it means they are not feeling challenged or engaged, or worse, bored. Students who love what is being presented are excited and hungry for knowledge. Our obligation as teachers and administrators is to provide that experience. How you go about it is an acquired skill. I urge you to wear your teaching hat 24/7. It does not mean that you will work those hours, but always be on the lookout for something new and exciting for the students.

Recently I had the privilege of leading a school of 1100 academically gifted students. You would think it would be the easiest job in the world, but you would be wrong. It was a daily chore making sure we had the necessary tools to provide an atmosphere conducive to learning. As a result, I believe it motivated me to become a much better administrator. In a hospital or college environment the administration is required to devote much of their time to resource procurement. In the Navy, you play a similar role as head of your assigned troops. For some odd reason that does not transfer well to the public school system in most cases. Attend your next local school board meeting and when they allow you to speak for two minutes ask them to provide you with a list of funds or resources they have provided to the schools since the last meeting.

For example, one day while reading the local paper I saw a story about a flood in the area where a creek overflowed and damaged a historic mill and blacksmith shop built in the late 18th century. It would be quite a task to return the building to working order. One of our math teachers at the Delaware Military Academy had a connection with the curator and offered our cadets to help clear the mill of mud as a community service project. While they were removing the mud, they came up with an exciting concept: develop an engineering class based on the mill and reconstruct the mill using the blacksmith shop to manufacture nails and 18th century tools. The class would be held on Saturday morning for eight weeks from 8-12.

As a result, the cadets cleaned the mill and participated in an outstanding engineering program, reconstructing the mill while encountering and overcoming real world engineering challenges. The curriculum was jointly written by our math teacher, Mark Stump, and the curator of the Mill, Tony Sheehan. They received the State Chamber of Commerce Super Stars in Education award for their efforts.

The point is, there are historic sites all over the country and partnering with them provides you with unique learning opportunities for students.

You will find that in public education, you are being denied resources. Whether it is in the form of funds, hardware, or texts, you are receiving only at a trickle in most states. If you happen to be overflowing with money and equipment, you are the exception.

Look for ways to compensate for this shortfall. Partner with city and state historical societies, parks and recreation programs, local colleges, hospitals, State Chambers, military bases—anywhere an opportunity exists to expand the horizon for your students.

One organization that is of significant value in identifying training opportunities is your state National Guard. The Adjutant General needs to be on your invitation list for annual inspections and formal military ceremonies. You may find that the AG can grant you access to many resources, such as rope courses, firing ranges, classrooms, military transportation opportunities (including C130 flights and helicopter demonstrations).

CHAPTER 13

. . . . ●. . . . .

Mentoring

What you leave behind is not what is engraved in stone monuments, but what is woven into the lives of others.

Pericles

We have a true crisis in education—public, private, and parochial. Simply put, it's the absence of leadership and mentors. Our universities and colleges graduate new teachers every year who are prepared to teach but not necessarily to lead.

I referred earlier in the text to the problem of classroom management. Although a major issue for new teachers, it may be addressed and taught. Leadership is much more difficult. Along with instruction, experience is also required. As a veteran, we need you among our ranks to provide mentorship for our students and inexperienced teachers. The values of honor, courage, and commitment are not part of the certification process. To veterans they are a way of life, allowing you to serve as outstanding role models.

You are aware I am sure of the vast numbers of youth who

run the streets and have little or no guidance. The media does a good job of reporting the crime and dropout statistics and if you were visiting the United States for the first time you would consider requesting combat pay. It is bad—not the end of the world by any means—but bad.

Speaking to you as a Master Chief with 25 years in the education system, I believe I am qualified to provide a veteran's perspective. Working with thousands of our youth from all walks of life, I discovered that the vast majority are wonderful, and they are asking for discipline and guidance. However, that doesn't make for enticing headlines.

At the DMA, we often had visitors tour the school, and afterward we held a brief question-and-answer period. The first question was typically, "What made you want to attend a military school?" The response was always centered around the discipline and the fact that there were fewer disruptions in class. The result: The Academy has one of the highest attendance rates of any school in the state—an indication that cadets are excited about coming to school, and want to learn and be successful.

The lowest performing schools are where discipline is out of control. I am convinced it is not about low income, race, single parent families, or the myriad excuses typically offered up to defend poor performance and poor leadership. Don't we have units in the military that reflect these demographic characteristics? Yet those units perform in an outstanding manner.

It is discouraging that we do not have more leaders who will stand up and take on the education challenge. As discussed earlier, moral courage is not an attribute widely exhibited in the higher levels of education administration. Administrators do not want to offend the school board or the legislators, so the apple cart is seldom tipped.

Mentoring is a main ingredient to the recipe for fixing the education problem, which in turn is the answer to keeping our society on track. Mentoring a student in many cases has come to mean only reading to them once a week. Granted, that is an exciting and important activity, but good mentoring is much more. It is a commitment to a young person and it does not stop after the school day is over. Many of my best mentoring moments have occurred on a Saturday morning run or on a field trip. Typically, mentees have questions in life skills and are appreciative of simple direction and attention.

There certainly is no shortage of mentees. If you do not have a student of your own to mentor, check with your school administrator to see if there is a school or district program where you may participate. Boys & Girls Clubs, Police Athletic Leagues, Community Centers, and Big Brother & Big Sister have mentorship programs. Mentoring is one of the most rewarding and most worthwhile investments of your time, love, and experience.

Currently I have 20-25 students who are in their 30s who remain in contact with me. They are doctors, military personnel, teachers, construction workers, housewives—they run the gamut of professions. Encountering them in everyday life is one of the great joys of being an educator.

Recently, while walking around the park for exercise, I saw a young man on a riding mower cutting the grass. Suddenly, he turned off the engine, jumped off the mower and ran over to me. "Commandant," he said, "remember me? I was one of your cadets and I graduated in 2006." Of course I remembered him. He proceeded to tell me he worked for the County Parks and Recreation Department and was a full-time student at a local college. He had been one of my challenges as well as a mentee, and it was great to see him as a successful student and citizen. The encounter made my day.

Periodically, I must still put on my mentor cap, and I do so happily. A memorable moment in that role occurred in the summer of 2009. I agreed to mentor a 9-year-old boy named Cyril. We did many activities together and he was eager to learn—canoeing, hiking, swimming, snorkeling, etc. Cyril successfully wore me out. I could handle the role as mentor, but being a 9-year-old playmate was not working out well for me. As a change of pace, we turned to reading. Both of our lives were transformed in the reading of *Treasure Island*. He and I set sail with Jim and the Squire after escaping from Black Dog and became mates with Long John Silver and Ben Gunn. We discovered treasure, fought off pirates, and had an exciting time of it. I look back on those few days as some of the most rewarding of my life and seldom does a week go by that I don't wish Cyril and I were hanging out with Long John. The immense joy of mentoring is beyond my ability to adequately describe.

Senator Tom Carper of Delaware is a retired Navy captain, Vietnam veteran and, for the more than 20 years that I have known him, a mentor. He is dedicated to his mentees and is an outstanding role model for the mentorship program. The Senator played a key role in supporting the founding and development of the Delaware Military Academy and the First State Military Academy. He is a true statesman and friend.

During one visit to our school, Senator Carper provided guidance that has been life-changing for me and my students. He shared a story with the graduating seniors about achieving success in life. A group of college students were visiting the Capitol Building, and during a question-and-answer session there was a question about the main ingredient in the recipe for success. Senator Carper's answer was so powerful I keep a sign over my desk with his exact quote: "Serve others."

CHAPTER 14

· · · · · · ●· · · · · · · · · ·

Fair Winds and Following Seas

Teaching, may I say, is the noblest profession of all in a democracy.

Kurt Vonnegut, Author

I have saved a short discussion on enthusiasm for one of your last impressions of *Carrier to Classroom*.

On board the Dwight D. Eisenhower, everything was IKE. We had an IKE Donald's sandwich shop, our ship's bulletin was the *IKE Bulletin*, and my TV show was IKE Beat. That even applied to our Marine First Sergeant. He was a typical Marine, professional and most of all, motivating. Every morning I would head up to the Hangar Bay to attend a Divisional Quarters. As I approached the Marine formation I would greet the Marines and say to the First Sergeant, "How are you this morning, First Sergeant?" His response was always the same: a booming "IKEstanding, Command Master Chief!" It always brought an immediate smile to my face. His enthusiasm regardless of the situation was always positive and inspiring, and I learned much from his leadership style.

Just as we did aboard the IKE, a teacher and a principal should implement **DPL 10 by displaying enthusiasm and providing humor to your students** as often as possible. For many of them it's the bright spot in their day and adds to the feeling that school is a good, fun, and safe place. If young people enjoy coming to school—our turf—it is our duty to provide a learning experience.

For example, as principal I had control of the school announcement system. In May – the last month of school—at the end of each day I would announce how many days were left before school would resume after summer vacation—130, 129, etc. The students all groaned, but in a positive way.

You can implement this in your school. For instance, if it begins to snow, announce that you will not cancel school because it is unsafe to drive and you have received parents' permission for a sleep over, "so we may continue classes until late in the evening."

In other words, lighten up. Attend extracurricular events, not just basketball and football games, but plays, dances, car washes, even sports practices. Display school pride, smile when you greet your students and, as stated before, assume they are up to something good. Prepare exciting and entertaining, not just informative, lesson plans.

As I come to the end of this narrative, I hope it has helped to convince you to pursue education as a possible career. The shortage of good teachers has reached crisis proportions. Economics plays a role, as do meddlesome school boards, poor administrative leadership, safety, and discipline. If you are not a military veteran and have not lived through a deployment away from your loved ones, stood duty, and been mired in bureaucracy for low pay, I understand why you might consider leaving the teaching profession. For the military veteran, however, teaching is a skill you are prepared to master—and the rewards are great.

Our youth need warriors to take up the challenge. You have a golden opportunity to join the ranks of a profession where every day you can go home a winner, knowing you have served others in the most positive way.

CHAPTER 15

· · · · · · · · ●● ● ● · · · · · · · · · ·

Closing The Deal

Education is the key to unlock the golden door of freedom.

Gen. George Washington

I decided to end this attempt at coaxing you as a military veteran to consider a career in education by providing several of the types of letters you can expect to receive as a reward for your efforts. I am relatively certain that many teachers have a cache of similar communications from grateful students, teachers, parents, and civic members. This is not about boasting or bragging; it is simply demonstrating the love and appreciation you can expect by serving the young people in our schools.

From a Parent
From: Captain, Delaware State Police
To: Commandant Baldwin, DMA
    Saturday night I was approached by my son and was informed that he would not be able to use the Opening Day tickets for the Baltimore Orioles game at Camden Yards. I asked him why not and what was the problem. He explained

he recently had been promoted to Platoon Leader and the date conflicted with the Navy Annual Inspection. My son did not think it was right to leave his troops behind for such an important evolution without their leadership present. What a great life lesson!! This was a significant father and son moment and I credit DMA for instilling this type of character development in my son. I attribute much of the credit to his Navy JROTC Instructors who focus on this type of education and traditional academics. It made my day.

For us to receive a letter from such an important member of the community was heart-warming. The captain was correct in indicating the lion's share of the credit should go to his son's Navy and Marine Corps Instructors.

From a Science Teacher
To: Commandant

I wanted to take a moment to say thank you for starting this wonderful school. My morning had a bumpy start but as I began my first class it got much better. All my cadets were working in groups. Some were sitting in the hall working quietly. Others were working in my room. Cadets asked questions about procedures and when finished with one task came to me to ask for more work. It was amazing. This continued all day in each class. To create a school with this type of culture is wonderful and a joy to come to work. Thank you

This teacher dedicated many hours to her students. She left a 17-year tenured union job to join DMA and worked there for 13 years before retiring.

From an alumnus and a Naval Academy Midshipman
To: Commandant

Commandant, today we finally received our Naval Academy rings. It is so hard to believe that I am already a second class and next year will be my firstie year here at the Academy. When I got my ring today you were the first person to pop into my head. I wouldn't be here today if weren't for you. As soon as I had interest in coming to the Naval Academy, you made sure that everything was done correctly and you fought for us like no one ever has before. You kept me motivated to complete the process and do everything to the best of my abilities. When we found out that I got in, you were there to rejoice with me, and it was the greatest feeling in the world. I hope you are doing well, and I think about you all the time. Hopefully I will be able to come up and see you at your new school. Thank you so much, Master Chief.

As your students move on in life you may receive many letters like this one. In few occupations are you privileged to have such a life-changing impact on individuals.

From a Student, in an essay on what he likes about the school
To: Commandant

The Commandant cares about all his cadets. He shows up to school every day and is seen throughout the day, everywhere in our small school. He knows all of our names and shows up at every organized event or activity. Sporting events, especially mine, cross country, where he yells my name and cheers for me. He is incessantly telling us to work hard and do not slack off with school work. Commandant is always trying to make the school better. Without him we would be just another school.

This student was very kind. I appreciate his observation that I was everywhere. As a Navy Master Chief I can leap tall buildings and I am faster than a locomotive, but I really can't be everywhere.

I hope what has been related to you in this narrative, coupled with the several testimonials, has made you eager to consider education as a possible career choice. I stand ready to welcome you aboard.

APPENDIX A

Deckplate Leadership

1. Always accept challenging assignments and situations. Be known as the one who gets it done.
2. It is okay to question an order and display apprehension. Remember, though, that proper procedure is to use the chain of command before you act.
3. Learn all the skills of an assigned position to gain the respect of your subordinates.
4. Use respectful language when dealing with people; never be demeaning or hurtful. If you slip, apologize, sincerely.
5. Praise in public, reprimand in private.
6. All students are great kids (soldiers, sailors, marines, airmen).
7. MAP -- daily performance composed of moral, academic, and physical activities.
8. Know your people.
9. Be known by your people.
10. Be enthusiastic.

APPENDIX B

Contact Information

1. Charles W. Baldwin cbcbaldwin19@gmail.com
2. Ross Sylvester ross@useed.org
3. John Moore john@useed.org

APPENDIX C

Websites

1. Delaware Military Academy www.demilacad.org
2. First State Military Academy www.fsmilitary.org
3. DANTES www.dantes.doded.mil/examinations
4. US Navy JROTC www.njrotc.mil/
5. US Marine Corps JROTC www.mcjrotc.marines.mil
6. US Air Force JROTC www.airuniversity.af.mil/holm-center/afjrotc
7. US Army JROTC www.usarmyjrotc.com/
8. (State) Department of Education for certification requirements
9. USEED (fund raising program) www.USEED.org

Dear Reader:

Thank you for taking the time to learn about Chuck Baldwin's vision to close the leadership gap in education. If you are a veteran, school board member, principal, a parent or an aspiring member of the education community, I hope you will implement some of the powerful ideas in the Command Master Chief's book.

One of the tools Chuck refers to is USEED, a predictable tool for crowdfunding. When we conceived of USEED at the

University of Delaware in 2011 we had a vision of a more engaging and productive future for education. We dreamed of a world where members of the community collaborate to deliver resources to enable students to engage in project-based learning. Since then we have partnered with some of the most innovative universities in the world, from Princeton to Australia National University and Arizona State University, to deliver this promised land for their students. Chuck urged us to expand our offering to high schools.

Like Chuck, I believe in unleashing and supporting the imagination of our young people. Even a small number of resources put in their hands can make a huge impact on society. For example, the internet was conceived by three friends at their Network Club at Van Nuys High School in 1961. They later brought it to fruition at UCLA. What incredible projects or adventures do you want to deliver for your students?

Please contact me at john@useed.org.

John Moore, Board Chairman, USEED

APPENDIX D

Frequently Asked Questions on Charter Schools

This should answer many of your charter school questions. If you find that it does not, please feel free to contact me at cbcbaldwin19@gmail.com

What is a charter school?

A charter school is an independently run public school granted greater flexibility in its operations, in return for greater accountability for performance. The "charter" establishing each school is a performance contract detailing the school's mission, program, students served, performance goals, and methods of assessment.

What is the difference between charter schools and other public schools?

Charter schools are public schools of choice, meaning that families choose them for their children. They operate with freedom from some of the regulations that are imposed upon district schools. Charter schools are accountable for academic results and for upholding the promises made in their charters. They must demonstrate performance in the areas of academic achievement, financial management, and organizational stability. If a charter school does not meet performance goals, it may be closed.

Are charter schools all the same?

No. Charter schools can vary a great deal in their design and in their results. Uncommon Schools, for instance, creates schools based on the principles and practices that have proven successful in producing significant academic gains at high-performing urban charter public schools across the country.

What is a charter management organization (CMO?)

A CMO offers wide-ranging support, including management and coaching of school leaders, professional development, staff recruitment, fundraising and more.

Among the areas a CMO supports are:

- K-12 Content Development
- Curriculum, K-8
- Development (Fundraising)
- Data Analytics
- Diversity
- External Relations

- Finance
- Human Resources
- Information Technology
- Marketing & Communications
- Performance Management
- Product Solutions
- Real Estate & Facilities
- School Management
- Recruitment
- Special Projects
- Talent Development
- Teach Like a Champion

Who authorizes charter schools?

This varies from state to state, depending on the state's charter law. Typical authorizers are the state, universities, and school districts.

Who can start a charter school?

Parents, community leaders, social entrepreneurs, businesses, teachers, school districts, and municipalities can submit a charter school proposal to their state's charter authorizing entity.

Who attends charter schools? Whom do they serve?

Nationwide, students in charter schools have demographic characteristics similar to students in the local public schools. In some states, charter schools serve significantly higher percentages of minority or low-income students than the traditional public schools. Charter schools accept students by random, public lottery.

How are charter schools funded?

As public schools, charter schools are tuition-free. They are funded according to enrollment levels and receive public funds on a per pupil basis. In many states, such as Alaska, Colorado, Minnesota, Delaware, and New Jersey, they receive less than 100 percent of the funds allocated to their traditional counterparts for school operations. In other states, such as California, additional funds or loans are made available to them. In most states, charters do not receive capital funds to support facility expenses. Charter schools are entitled to federal categorical funding for which their students are eligible, such as Title I and Special Education monies. Federal legislation provides grants to help charters with start-up costs.

How can I enroll my child in a charter school?

Each school admits students through a random lottery and every state has laws that differ regarding the enrollment process. A state charter may differ from a district charter. Check with your State Department of Education for requirements.

Do teachers need to be certified to work at a charter school?

Again, certification requirements vary from state to state. In New Jersey and Delaware all teachers must be certified, and local universities offer teachers alternate routes to secure their teaching credentials.

APPENDIX E

Navy JROTC Instructor Application Information

For obvious reasons, I selected the information on the Navy high school program. Each branch has its own requirements and I encourage you to use the contact information provided and research your military service.

NAVY JUNIOR RESERVE OFFICER TRAINING CORPS

The NJROTC program:

- Promotes patriotism
- Develops informed and responsible citizens
- Develops respect for constructed authority
- Develops a high degree of personal honor, self-reliance, individual discipline and leadership
- Promotes an understanding of the basic elements and need for national security
- Provides information on the military services as a possible career

- Promotes community service
- Develops leadership potential
- Provides an alternative to gangs
- Promotes high school completion
- Provides incentive to live healthy and drug free

Q. What are the student enrollment eligibility requirements?

A. A student must:

- Be enrolled in and attending a regular course of instruction in a grade 9 through 12 at the school hosting the unit.
- Be physically qualified to participate fully in the physical education program of the host school.
- Be selected by the NJROTC instructor with the approval of the school principal or his/her representative.
- Maintain acceptable standards of academic achievement and an academic standing that warrants at least normal progression leading to graduation.
- Maintain acceptable standards of conduct.
- Comply with specified personal grooming standards. Common sense and good judgment apply to the attainment of these standards.
- Under the secondary school open enrollment policy and when desired by the principal of the host school, students in grades 9-12 who are otherwise ineligible for regular NJROTC enrollment may enroll as special NJROTC cadets. Special NJROTC cadets may participate in school approved NJROTC activities, be called naval cadets, wear the uniform, participate as cadet officers, and go on field trips and orientation visits to military installations. Special NJROTC students may not, however, be counted with that number required to maintain a NJROTC unit. Any special equipment or

additional staff that may be needed to instruct special NJROTC students is provided by the school.

Q. What are the benefits of NJROTC?

A. Benefits include:

- Approximately 60 percent of the NJROTC graduating seniors continue to higher education.
- NJROTC teaches students the basic elements and need for national security and their personal obligations as Americans.
- The program enhances the image of the military in the eyes of the community by providing a chance for success to the nation's youth.
- While the training is along military lines, it encourages initiative and individuality and develops natural gifts, self-control, character, responsibility, and qualities of integrity, loyalty, and dedication.
- Cadets develop self-esteem from belonging to NJROTC.
- NJROTC cadets are better behaved, have higher attendance, and are role models for the avoidance of substance abuse, graduate at a higher rate, and are an excellent source of service accessions.
- The values, principles, and self-discipline taught in NJROTC promotes positive, productive behaviors and provides a support structure that is critical in helping cadets avoid the use of drugs.
- The NJROTC program is motivational in encouraging cadets to graduate from high school.
- Cadets presenting evidence of successful completion of at least three years of NJROTC are entitled to advanced promotion to paygrade E-3 upon initial enlistment in an active or reserve component of the Navy or Air Force and receive paygrade E-2 in the Army or Marine Corps.

- Cadets accepted for enlistment who provide evidence of successful completion of two years of a NJROTC program are entitled to be enlisted in paygrade E-2 (except in the Marine Corps and Air Force).
- Senior Naval Science Instructor is authorized to nominate a maximum of three eligible cadets each year to compete for Naval Academy appointments.
- In addition to the three nominations above to the Naval Academy, administrators of host schools designated as Distinguished Units with Academic Honors may nominate three eligible NJROTC cadets as candidates for appointment to the Naval Academy, the Military Academy, and U.S. Air Force Academy.

Q. What subjects are included in the curriculum?

A. The subjects include:

- CITIZENSHIP -- Instills values and responsibilities of good citizenship.
- NAVAL ORIENTATION -- A basic introduction to the Navy -- its customs, traditions, and way of life.
- NAVAL OPERATIONS/ORGANIZATION -- Familiarizes the student with national strategy and naval forces, daily military operations, training, exercises, drills, and shipboard organization.
- NAVAL HISTORY -- History of the United States Navy from the colonial period to the present.
- NAVIGATION -- An introduction to piloting and celestial navigation.
- SEAMANSHIP -- An introduction to seamanship, including anchoring and mooring, ship handling, small boats, weather, ship construction, and steering, and propulsion systems.

- LEADERSHIP -- An ongoing study of the principles and practical application of leadership with emphasis on providing opportunities for students to exercise and develop their own leadership abilities.
- NAUTICAL ASTRONOMY -- A study of astronomy and its application to celestial navigation.
- ELECTRONICS -- An introduction to electronics as the basis for shipboard radar, sonar, communications, and guidance systems.
- OCEANOGRAPHY – A study of the collection and dissemination of hydrographic and navigational data from the world's oceans.
- DRILLS, COMMANDS, AND CEREMONIES -- Includes individual, squad, platoon, and company close order drill, rotation of command, physical fitness, personnel inspections, and parade in company review.

Q. Who are the NJROTC Instructors?

A. NJROTC instructors may be:

Retired Navy, Marine Corps, or Coast Guard commissioned officers, warrant officers, and enlisted personnel, E-6 through O-6, who have served a minimum of 20 years of active duty. The Head of the Department of Naval Science at a school hosting an NJROTC program is called the Senior Naval Science Instructor (SNSI). The SNSI is the commissioned officer or Warrant Officer (with degree) employed by the school. Enlisted personnel or warrant officers and LDOs without degrees employed by the school in the NJROTC program are called Naval Science Instructors (NSI). Warrant Officers or LDOs with a bachelor's degree may also apply to the school for employment as an NSI. Either the SNSI or NSI must have retired from the United States Navy. The minimum education requirement for SNSIs is a bachelor's degree from an accredited college or university.

Who are the NJROTC Instructor

NJROTC instructors are sea service personnel certified by NSTC and employed by school districts hosting NJROTC units. The Department Head of Naval Science at a school hosting an NJROTC program is called the Senior Naval Science Instructor (SNSI). The SNSI is the commissioned officer or Warrant Officer (with degree) employed by the school. Enlisted personnel or warrant officers and LDOs without degrees employed by the school in the NJROTC program are called Naval Science Instructors (NSI). Warrant Officers or LDOs with a baccalaureate degree may also apply to the school for employment as an NSI. At each unit, either the SNSI or NSI must be from the United States Navy.

To be eligible for certification as an instructor, applicants must:

- Have at least 20 years of active duty in the Navy, Marine Corps, or Coast Guard as commissioned officers in grades W-2 through O-6, or as non-commissioned officers in grades E-6 through E-9; and
- Be in a retired or Fleet Reserve status not more than six years; or
- Have been approved for retirement benefits within the past six years under the Temporary Early Retirement Authority with 15 to 19 years of active duty service in the Navy; or
- Be retired Naval Reserve members who are not yet receiving retirement benefits (i.e. "gray area" retirees); or
- Have been approved for retirement benefits from the Navy, Marine Corps, or Coast Guard for a medical disability within the past six years; and
- Have attained the following educational degrees:

- Senior Naval Science Instructor - Bachelor's degree from accredited college or university recognized by the U.S. Department of Education.
- Naval Science Instructor - Associate's degree from accredited college or university recognized by the Department of Education, or attainment of that degree within five years of initial employment as a result of the FY 2007 National Defense Authorization Act (NDAA). Instructors already employed must complete the requirement by June 15, 2012, to retain instructor certification.

If you do not already have an associate's degree, a great way to start would be to access your SMART transcripts and have them reviewed for college credit. In addition, you could work with your education officer to CLEPP (College Level Examination Program) as many courses as possible. *You may be closer to a degree than you think!*

Useful Information: Navy College issues credits based on the authority that the individual sailor/Marine has already proven he/she can work, supervise, manage, and complete the necessary tasks and skills at the higher rank level, but is unable to be selected for the higher grade via the selection boards due to high exam multiples, promotion ceilings, etc. The Navy/Marine Corps feels that if the sailor/Marine is scoring high enough to pass the exam and has proven he/she has the knowledge to operate at the next level, credit should be given.

To obtain this higher certification, military members need to access the BUPERS website and print an exam profile sheet for the next higher pay grade. Upon obtaining the profile sheet, members have it "certified to be a true copy" (this can be done by a supervisor of higher rank) and mail that to the Navy College Center at https://www.navycollege.navy.mil and they will evaluate and award credit for the next higher grade, even though actual promotion was not attained for the next higher grade. Navy College Center is very good and will usually take two weeks to post on the member's SMART transcript.

To update other information on the SMART, go to https://smart.navy.mil.

Once employed, you will be required to attend a Navy-sponsored instructor training seminar. The state in which you accept employment may have additional requirements you must meet. Specific instructor qualification requirements will remain the decision of local school officials.

NJROTC instructors are conspicuous military representatives in the civilian community. As such, they are expected to uphold traditional military standards of decorum and personal appearance. Instructors are required to wear the prescribed uniform while instructing and at other appropriate times. Cost of uniform acquisition and maintenance is borne by the individual instructor. Attention to the maintenance of proper uniforms and personal appearance is essential. Instructors must meet the Navy screening tables for weight by height or the percent of body fat standards set in OPNAVINST 6110.1H.

What are the duties of the NJROTC Instructors?

The SNSIs shall perform those duties pursuant to current regulations, policies, and procedures as established by NSTC and the host school. The SNSI also reports to the NJROTC area manager for administrative and logistical support. The NSI also teaches naval science courses, assists the SNSI, and shares workload duties as assigned by the SNSI. In addition to the specific duties listed below, they may perform those collateral duties normally performed by and rotated among other faculty members, providing such duties do not interfere with the administration and operation of the NJROTC program.

Specific duties and responsibilities of the SNSI and NSI include:

- Teaching the prescribed three- or four-year Naval Science curriculum.
- Instructing in military drill.
- Counseling students in the NJROTC program.
- Writing/updating lesson plans for the NJROTC curriculum and other lesson preparation requirements.
- Mentoring cadets and assisting with higher education or employment opportunities and goals.
- Requisitioning all government furnished equipment (including uniforms, training aids, books, drill rifles, air rifles, organizational equipment).
- Arranging for cleaning and tailoring of uniforms.
- Surveying old and worn uniforms and other government property.
- Performing simple preventive maintenance of training aids and devices.
- Inventory control of all government furnished equipment/materials (including annual wall-to-wall inventory).
- Ensuring proper physical security of all government furnished equipment/materials.
- Planning extracurricular activities for the NJROTC unit (including color/honor guard ceremonies, drill team and rifle team competitions, field trips, basic leadership training, ship cruises, etc.).
- Preparing periodic reports on program administration and logistics.
- Keeping abreast of developments and organization changes within the Navy.
- Assessing unit progress to assure NJROTC program objectives are met.
- Attending Navy-sponsored training to keep abreast of current requirements of program management.
- Taking courses of instruction to improve teaching abilities.

- Establishing rapport with school counselors and faculty members.
- Making annual presentations of the NJROTC program to students at feeder schools for the purpose of recruiting new cadets into the program.
- Maintaining financial accounts and operating budget.
- Preparing financial vouchers to the Navy for reimbursement of expenditures to the school in support of the NJROTC program.
- Establishing contact with civic groups to obtain their recognition and support of the NJROTC program.

How are applicants certified as NJROTC Instructors?

NJROTC Instructor Certification Boards are convened semi-annually by the Naval Service Training Command (NSTC), usually in the spring and fall. Dates for the convening of the board and the application due date are published on the NJROTC web site: https://www.njrotc.navy.mil. The Navy Personnel Command (NAVPERSCOM) requires specific information 30 days prior to the convening date of the board to ensure the applicant's service record will be available for review. NSTC (NJROTC) furnishes this information to NAVPERSCOM based on information contained in the NJROTC Instructor Certification Application (NSTC CD Form 1533/2 (12-06)). The board is normally composed of five officers and one recorder, and is usually in session for one week. The board will review the complete service record and NJROTC instructor application package. Results may be obtained by visiting the NJROTC website after authorization to release the results has been granted. Applicants will be individually notified via letter after the board has adjourned. The instructor certification will remain valid for three years except for applicants who have been retired more than three years from active duty. While employed, certification is extended on a year-to-year basis. Instructors whose employment at a school ends through no fault of their own (e.g., unit closure) or to accept another position will retain their certification for one year from the date of termination. If not reemployed in the program within the one-year period, application for recertification may be made to NSTC (NJROTC) within six years following termination of employment at a unit. Special boards may be convened by NSTC if necessary on a case-by-case basis to consider certification requests or decertification actions.

A special board is convened to consider decertification when information regarding a prior screened applicant or actions of an NJROTC instructor indicates that, in the best interest of the NJROTC program, immediate action is necessary to consider continued certification.

What is the application procedure?

Eligible sea service personnel may apply for a three-year certification as a SNSI or NSI. If not employed within that period, applicants may request an additional three-year certification. However, applicants must be certified and employed within six years of active duty retirement. Personnel who have been medically retired with less than 20 years of active duty service are not eligible until they are receiving permanent retired pay. Active duty personnel within one year of retirement may apply for certification.

Applicants must complete the NJROTC Instructor Certification Application (NSTC CD Form 1533/2 (12-06)) and NJROTC Instructor Applicant Checklist (NSTC CD Form 1533/14 (12-06)). These forms may be obtained from the NJROTC Web Site at inst_app_required_forms.html. Note the requirement to answer two questions, either handwritten or typed, in essay form. The following must also be included with the application and checklist:

Current photograph (not more than one year old). The

uniform for this photograph shall be khaki or the current Navy working uniform to provide maximum photographic clarity. (Navy E-6 applicants may also wear summer white or winter working blues, depending on the season). Coast Guard applicants are to be photographed in a uniform comparable to that specified for Navy applicants. The photograph shall display a full-length three-quarter view of the applicant in the prescribed uniform, uncovered, with the left shoulder forward, against a plain contrasting background, in a size approximately 4 inches in width and 5 inches in height. Background shall be flat and provide sufficient contrast to highlight details of the uniform. When an authorized Navy photographic laboratory or an alternate support facility is unavailable, any photograph that complies, as closely as possible, with the requirements specified above is acceptable. For officers, these are the same requirements specified for official file photographs.

A Navy interview is required for the certification process. The applicant must contact the NJROTC area manager nearest his/her location to schedule the interview. The NJROTC Area Managers Directory may be accessed on the website: http://www.njrotc.navy.mil/mgdgeo.html. The applicant must make all arrangements and bear any costs of the interview (including travel). However, the area manager will make every effort to schedule the interview as close as possible to the applicant's location. Active duty applicants assigned overseas may ask a senior naval officer at their location to conduct the interview and may obtain the interview form from NSTC (NJROTC Instructor Administration) or any area manager's office. The results of the interview must be forwarded to NSTC by the interviewer only.

Coast Guard applicants must ask Coast Guard officials to provide a copy of the applicant's service record for review by the certification board. Coast Guard applicants must write to Commanding Officer, U.S. Coast Guard (CGPC-adm-3), 4200 Wilson Blvd., Suite 1000, Arlington, VA 22203-1804, cite the Privacy Act, and request that the service record be mailed directly to: Naval Service Training Command, NJROTC Program, ATTN Instructor Administration, 250 Dallas St., Suite A, Pensacola, FL 32508-5268. The service record copy will be returned to the applicant after review by the NJROTC Instructor Certification Board.

Marine Corps applicants must provide Part I - Basic Information and Part II - Education of the NJROTC Instructor Application, a copy of their Marine Corps Certification letter. Those who have previously served or are currently serving as instructors with the Marine Corps JROTC must also provide Instructor Evaluations covering the last three years of employment as an instructor. If an instructor has worked for less than three years, he or she must provide evaluations for the period of employment. If formal instructor evaluations are not available, a letter from a school official documenting performance must be provided.

Marine Corps Junior Reserve Officers Training Corps (MCJROTC) Certification can be obtained from Head Training Programs Branch, Training and Education Division C462JR, MCCDC, 1019 Elliott Rd., Quantico, VA 22134-5012, or telephone at (703) 784-3705/DSN 278-3705.

Naval Reserve personnel must also include the STATEMENT of SERVICE for NAVAL RESERVE RETIREMENT.

How do certified instructors seek employment?

Upon certification as an instructor in the NJROTC program, personnel will be furnished a letter of certification. Current vacancy information may be obtained at the following website: https://netfocus2.netc.navy.mil/Jrotc/inst_vac.asp. NJROTC area managers are available to assist prospective instructors in securing employment. **However, it is the responsibility of the individual to establish contact with host schools and to arrange for employment interviews.** The cost of travel to/ from employment interviews must be borne by the individual or school. A list of all certified applicants is provided to area managers and school officials with vacancies periodically. The applicant is encouraged to provide updated information as needed to the NJROTC Instructor Administration office by calling (850) 452-9510 or 9511, or email pnsc_cnet.njrotc@ navy.mil.

What is the NJROTC Instructor/Host School relationship?

In order to achieve maximum coordination between the NJROTC unit and other academic departments, the staff of the Department of Naval Science shall be given full membership in the high school's faculty in appropriate ranks and be accorded the rights and privileges of faculty members. The SNSI is the Naval Science Department Head, and is accorded the same privileges as other host school department heads. It is hoped that the SNSI encourages the high school authorities, when appropriate, to use the naval science staff members on faculty committees so their services may be utilized in the same manner as are the services of other members of the faculty.

The selection and employment of retired officer and enlisted personnel for duty with NJROTC units and relief therefrom are functions of the local institution. Although retired personnel hired as NJROTC instructors are employees of the school, and are responsible to the school administrators, NSTC retains ultimate responsibility and authority for the NJROTC program. Therefore, it is expected that instructors will meet requirements and standards prescribed by NSTC, as well as those of the host school administration.

All traditional military courtesies and respect will be accorded SNSIs/NSIs according to their rank or rate. However, they are in a civilian status while employed in the NJROTC program.

Is there a special training or course for NJROTC instructors?

The New Instructor Orientation Training (NIOT) seminar course of instruction to indoctrinate new SNSIs and NSIs is held annually, normally the end of July. All instructors are required to attend this orientation training during the first year of their employment to complete the certification process.

Schools are asked to provide travel funds to the instructor. A letter will be sent to the instructor announcing the training and indicating the amount of per diem/travel expenses authorized. Schools will be reimbursed by NSTC upon submittal of a Wide Area Work Flow (WAWF) claim.

Personnel still on active duty (or terminal leave) at the time of the orientation training who have signed a contract with the school may be issued Temporary Additional Duty orders by their command, utilizing NSTC accounting data.

The NJROTC New Instructor Orientation Training prerequisite online course at Navy Knowledge Online (NKO) must be completed prior to the NIOT seminar.

Additional courses will be provided to enhance professional skills and development online and at Area InService Training throughout the year as prescribed by NSTC or for advanced certification.

How are Instructor salaries determined?

Minimum Salary: Personnel shall receive a salary at least equal to the difference between their retired pay and the active duty pay and allowances, excluding incentive pay, which they would receive if ordered to active duty. The institution is the employing agency and shall pay the full salary due the employee. The school will be reimbursed half of the minimum salary for each instructor.

Minimum Salary Changes: The minimum salary for instructors normally changes once a year. The January adjustment is based on changes in active duty pay and allowances and retired CPI adjustments. NSTC CD will provide individual instructors with written notification of changes as they occur. The instructor will notify the school.

Method of Salary Reimbursement Computation: This shall be based on a 30-day month. When employment begins or ends during the month, pay entitlement will be 1/30 of the minimum monthly salary for each day of employment. For example: An instructor hired on the 10th day of any month, including February, shall be paid for 21 days (30 days less nine days not employed = 21). The computation for a minimum monthly salary of $2,557.52 divided by 30 = $85.25 x 21 = $1,790.25 (minimum to be paid by school). Reimbursement by the Navy to the school would be $1,790.25 divided by 2 = $895.13. The Navy is prohibited from reimbursing the school for personnel still on active duty, i.e., terminal leave.

Relocation Costs: If relocation is necessary to secure employment, it is the responsibility of selected instructors to relocate at their own expense to the area where they are hired. The Navy has no objection if the school provides reimbursement for all or part of these expenses. This subject should be discussed during the employment interview.

Benefits: Instructors in the NJROTC program normally receive the same benefits (sick leave, vacation, holiday, retirement, etc.) afforded other teachers in the school district. It is recommended, however, that such benefits be thoroughly discussed in the employment interview.

Employment Notification: Applicants must notify their area manager of initial date of employment. However, to expedite NJROTC instructor pay computations upon employment, the following documentation must be forwarded to the NJROTC instructor pay desk:

1. A copy of discharge DD214 (MEMBER COPY-4).

2. A copy of your current Retiree Account Statement (RAS) from Defense Finance Accounting Service (DFAS), Cleveland, Ohio.
3. Form DD2767, Dec 1998 (JROTC Instructor Annual Certification of Pay and Data Form).
4. Form DD 2754, Dec 1998 (JROTC Instructor Pay Certification Worksheet for Entitlement Computation). For those instructors who are authorized to draw Basic Allowance for Housing (BAH) with dependents, a copy of your marriage certificate/license or final divorce decree should accompany the DD 2754.

Mail all documents to: Naval Service Training Command, NJROTC Program, ATTN Code CD211, 250 Dallas St., Suite A, Pensacola, FL 32508-5268. For further assistance, call the Instructor Pay desk at DSN 922-9490 or (850) 452-9490.

Additional Duties: The primary responsibility of the SNSI and NSI employed by an institution with an NJROTC unit shall be that of instruction and administration of the NJROTC program. Compensation for duties assigned by the institution other than NJROTC duties shall be resolved by the NJROTC instructor and the local institution officials on a separate contractual basis.

APPENDIX F

FSMA School Profile

First State Military Academy (School Year 2015-16)

District:	First State Military Academy
Address:	355 West Duck Creek Road, P.O. Box 888, Clayton DE 19938
Principal:	Patrick Gallucci
AYP:	Not Applicable

Telephone: (302) 223-2150
Web: www.fsmilitaryacademy.org/

School Demographics

Fall Enrollment		Enrollment by Race/Ethnicity		Other Student Characteristics	
	2016		**2016**		**2016**
Grade 9	142	African American	24.3%	English Language Learner	0.5%
Grade 10	60	Asian	1.0%	Low Income	35.6%
Total	202	Hispanic/Latino	9.4%	Special Education	19.3%
		White	61.4%	Enrolled for Full Year	N/A
Recently Arrived ELL Stude		Multi-Racial	4.0%		
		2			

Number of Students Not Tested on ELA Assessment	0

No Data Available

Delaware
Department of
Education

118

Exemplary Programs

First State Military Academy is committed to making a positive difference in the lives of our students. We utilize two proven programs to enhance future success. We accomplish this by setting high academic expectations for all students. We maintain a strong school culture of trust, respect, and responsibility, and set high standards for teacher performances. We commit to the New Tech Network and problem-solving, project-based learning which leads to greater successes in college acceptance, college persistence, and career readiness. We are using our concepts to shape the lives of our students. We will forever change their future as we introduce them to valuable skills and attributes necessary to succeed in the 21st century. We are making a difference in the lives of our students, one day at a time.

Student - School Safety and Discipline

Number of Reported Offenses (2015-2016)

	School	District	State
School Crimes (Title 14, Delaware Code, §4112)	6	6	1612
Department of Education (DOE) Offenses	38	38	26031
All School Safety Policy in Place	N/A		

Suspensions and Expulsions

	2016
Number of Suspensions	82
Number of Expulsions	4
Count of Students Suspended/Expelled	38
September 30 Enrollment	202
Percent of Students Suspended/Expelled	19%
District Percentage	19%
State Percentage	13%

Percent Days Present (2015-2016)

92.16%

7.84%

- ■ Percent Days Present
- ■ Percent days not present

Our Staff

Number of Instructional Staff

	2016
Teachers	10
Pupil Support	3
Total	13

Staff by Race/Ethnicity

	2016
American Indian	0.0%
African American	7.7%
Asian American	0.0%
Hispanic	0.0%
White	92.3%

Staffing Ratios

	2016
Students Per Teacher	20
Students Per Administrator	202
Students Per Instructional Staff	20
Students Per Pupil Support Staff	76
School Staff Per Administrator	15

Staff Qualifications

Percentage of Classes Taught by Highly Qualified Teachers (2015-2016)

	Total Classes	% Highly Qualified	% Not Highly Qualified
English	10	100.0%	0.0%
Arts	1	100.0%	0.0%
Foreign Languages	6	0.0%	100.0%
Science	10	60.0%	40.0%
Mathematics	11	72.7%	27.3%
Civics & Government	8	100.0%	0.0%
History	3	100.0%	0.0%

Years of Teaching Experience (2015-2016)

80.0%

10.0%

10.0%

- ■ 4 years or Less
- ■ 10-14 Years
- ■ 15-19 Years

Education Level

	2016
Percent with Masters Degree and Above	53.8%

Curriculum Highlights

New Tech Network creates an innovative learning environment through a proven school model, a project-based learning platform, and powerful professional development. Technology supports our innovative approach to instruction and culture. With one-to-one computing and the latest in collaborative learning technology, every student becomes a self-directed learner who no longer has to rely on teachers or textbooks for knowledge and direction.

The goal of MCJROTC is to develop leadership, character and citizenship skills, and enhance self-discipline through a challenging four-year leadership education program. Our training is conducted to encourage initiative and individuality, to develop natural gifts, to teach self-control, to develop personal character, responsibility, and qualities of integrity, loyalty, and dedication. The leadership skills the students will learn in four years at First State Military Academy are more than most adults will experience in a lifetime.

(-1-)				
	ELA	Math	ELA Goal	Math Goal

Delaware
Department of Education

School Salary Allocation

Instructional Service		Instructional Support		Instructional vs. Support (2015-2016)
	2016		2016	
Teachers	63.9%	Administration	12.7%	
Pupil Support	15.2%	Secretaries	5.1%	79.1%
Total	79.1%	Food Services	3.1%	20.9%
		Total	20.9%	

Instructional Service
Instructional Support

For further information and detailed reports, visit

http://profiles.doe.k12.de.us

or contact your local school district office.

Glossary: http://profiles.doe.k12.de.us/glossary.aspx

Delaware Department of Education
John G. Townsend Building
401 Federal Street, Suite #2
Dover, Delaware, 19901 - 3639
Phone: (302) 735-4000

120

APPENDIX G

DMA School Profile

School Safety and Discipline		

Number of Reported Offenses (2015-16)

	School	District	State
School Crimes (Title 14, Delaware Code, §4112)	3	98	802
Department of Education (DOE) Offenses	1	1,468	13,016
All School Safety Policy in Place	N/A		

Info | Details

Suspensions and Expulsions

	2015-16
Number of Suspensions	24
Number of Expulsions	0
Count of Students Suspended/Expelled	20
September 30 Enrollment	564
Percent of Students Suspended/Expelled	4%
District Percentage	12%
State Percentage	13%

Info | Details

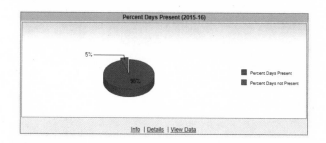

Percent Days Present (2015-16)

5%

95%

■ Percent Days Present
■ Percent Days not Present

Info | Details | View Data

Student Achievement

SAT: Average Scores for the Class of (2014-15)

	School	District	State
Math	487	511	449
Critical Reading	501	507	449
Writing	475	495	429
Total	1,463	1,513	1,327

Info | Details

11th Grade School Day SAT Reasoning Test (2014-15)

	School	District	State
Math	468	485	435
Critical Reading	474	492	441
Writing	465	476	422
Total	1,407	1,453	1,298
Participation	99%	93%	93%

Info | Details

Advanced Placement (AP)

	2015-16
Advanced Placement Courses	10
No. of Students Enrolled	72
No. of Exams Taken	102
Total No. of Exams Passed	54

Info | Details

Percentage of Students Meeting State Standards (2015-16)

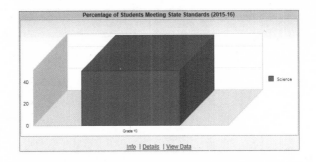

Info | Details | View Data

Graduation Rate - ESEA 4 Year Adjusted

StudentAccountability	2013-14 2013-14-ESEA	2014-15 2014-15-ESEA
All Students	99.2%	97.9%
American Indian	100.0%	100.0%
African American	100.0%	93.3%
Asian American	100.0%	100.0%
Hispanic	100.0%	88.9%
White	99.1%	99.1%
Multi-Racial	100.0%	
Special Education	100.0%	100.0%
Low Income	100.0%	90.0%

Info | Details

122

This book is dedicated to
to my beautiful Italian wife
Salvatorica (Rica)
and her beautiful sister
Nina

Thank you to my family
Antonella, William, Anthony, Monika,
Marisa, Cyril, Matteo, Mira, Milania,
David, Elizabeth, Stephanie, Cullan, Harlow, Brandon, Tessa

To my lifetime friend
Bill Spiese
Who now knows what I do for a living.

A special thank you for their kind words,
support, and friendship
to
Dr. Robert Andrzejewski, Educator, Superintendent
John Moore, Entrepreneur and Board Chair USEED
Tom Hutchison, LCDR, USNR, Businessman, Adventurer

And a special thank you to the 8th Master
Chief Petty Officer of the Navy
MCPON John Hagan
USN Ret.
For his service to our country in leading
our great Navy into the 21st century.

Editing and mentoring was provided by my friend Robert Yearick

ABOUT THE AUTHOR

Charles Baldwin is a retired U.S. Navy Command Master Chief, former Navy Junior Reserve Officer Training Corps Instructor, Middle School Principal, High School Principal, and Co-Founder and Commandant of the Delaware Military Academy, Retired. He now serves as a part-time education consultant, motivational speaker, mountain climber, and Italian language interpreter. The Master Chief is a Vietnam and Persian Gulf veteran. He holds a Master's Degree in School Leadership and Instruction from Wilmington University.

His passion is education and mentoring young men and women. He is an active participant in the Delaware Leadership Initiative, Delaware Youth Leadership Initiative, Hugh O'Brian

Youth Leadership program (HOBY) and is a consultant and fund-raiser for the First State Military Academy Marine Corps JROTC Academy in Clayton, Del. Charles serves as a Commissioner on the Delaware Commission of Veteran Affairs, representing Vietnam Veterans.

For his work in education he was awarded a Tribute by the US Senate in the 111th Congress sponsored by Senator Thomas Carper, and the Distinguished Service Medal from the Delaware Adjutant General.

He and his wife of 43 years, Rica, have two children, Antonella Pullella of Wilmington, Del., and Bm2 (SW) William Baldwin, serving in the Navy as a Recruit Division Commander at Recruit Training Center, Great Lakes, Ill. They are the proud grandparents of Marisa, Matteo, Mira, Milania Pullella, and Cyril Baldwin.

Charles and Rica reside in Wilmington for a portion of the year and spend the remainder in Ala' Dei Sardi, Sardinia, Italy.